Starting Secondary School Science

First published 2002
exclusively for WHSmith by

Hodder & Stoughton Educational
338 Euston Road
London
NW1 3BH

A CIP record for this book is available from the British Library.

Text: Graham Peacock

Typeset by Fakenham Photosetting Ltd, Fakenham, Norfolk.

ISBN 0 340 84738 7

Printed and bound in Spain by Graphycems.

Contents

Introduction

The move from primary to secondary school can be quite an overwhelming experience. You will encounter completely new subject areas and a whole range of new topics and concepts, as well as new teachers and a new and much bigger school environment. Some people say it is like changing from a big fish in a small pond (primary school) into a small fish in a big pond (secondary school)!

The books in this *Starting Secondary School* series will help bridge the gap between primary and secondary school and ease the transition between the two.

From a big fish in a small pond to a small fish in a big pond.

This introduction will answer some of the most frequently asked questions about starting secondary school.

What are lessons like at secondary school?

You'll probably be placed in a tutor group, which meets for registration each day with the same teacher, and you are likely to stay with this group for quite a few subjects. In some subjects, like English and maths, you may be placed in a set with other children of similar ability to make it easier for you and the rest to work at a similar pace.

The timetable is very important at secondary school. Lessons are for set times and there may be a bell signalling the end of each lesson. Different subjects are taught in different rooms and you will be told and shown where to go. It is important to get to know your timetable as quickly as possible and to know where to go for each lesson. You could fill in the blank timetable at the end of this book to help you.

Will I be able to find my way around?

Life at secondary school may seem very different to life at primary school at first. For a start, everything seems much bigger. The buildings are bigger, the students are bigger – and there are more of them! A common fear is of getting lost or not being able to find your way around. Don't worry. Your teachers will make sure you know where to go and there's always someone you can ask. Remember – if in doubt about anything, ask! Nobody will mind if you do. Everyone at the school is there to help you, and to help you to do your best.

How do secondary schools work?

Each subject follows a scheme of work, which has been agreed by each subject department and will be based on Key Stage 3 of the National Curriculum. You will mostly study the same subjects you did at primary school. The main difference is that you will have different teachers to help you. You will also begin to study at least one modern foreign language, usually French or German. The choice of languages available differs from school to school.

What about tests?

It is likely that you will have more tests and assessments at secondary school than you did at primary school. You will usually be told when these are to take place and will be given plenty of time to revise and prepare for them. If you are sensible and do your homework, these tests should not worry you at all.

What about homework?

Homework is set in accordance with an agreed timetable so that you will have different subjects to deal with on different evenings. In your first year this will not be too time-consuming. A good tip is to do your homework as soon as you can, rather than leave it till the last minute and rush it. And remember to take it to school with you on the day you are supposed to hand it in!

How will I cope with the extra freedom that I will have at secondary school?

A lot of emphasis is placed on being independent and responsible in secondary school. Thinking ahead and being organised will help you a lot. Always get to your lessons and take everything you need with you. The teachers will tell you what you need to bring to each lesson.

How will my parents know what I am doing at school?

Most schools use a homework diary in which homework is recorded and some schools ask parents to sign these regularly to show that they have read them. It is important that your parents know what your are doing at school. This is one way of helping them find out. Don't forget to talk to them too! Your school will probably also have regular open evenings when your parents will be invited to school to talk to your teachers and discuss your progress.

What will science be like at secondary school?

At primary school you will have been familiar with science being taught by your class teacher. At secondary school you will study many of the same sorts of things at a different level. Often, one teacher will teach science, but sometimes you will have up to three different science teachers.

- You will begin to learn that science is divided into physics, chemistry and biology.
- You will learn many more facts about science.
- You will be expected to design and carry out experiments even more carefully than you did in primary school.
- You will carry out experiments with equipment, which will need to be used safely. At secondary school you may use equipment like eye protection goggles when handling chemicals and hot liquids.
- You will be expected to use equipment more accurately. Weighing balances and digital thermometers might measure more precisely than the equipment you have been used to in primary school.
- You will be expected to write up experiments, often using headings such as 'method', 'diagram', 'results' and 'conclusion'.
- You will learn how to take notes from what the teacher says and include these in your exercise books.
- You will be taught how to predict what is going to happen in an experiment and how to make sense of what does happen.
- You will be expected to be able to use reference books, like a science dictionary and encyclopaedia.

How will this book help me?

All of the things in this book are designed to help you with work you will be doing at secondary school in science. Work through the units in any order you wish. In the Glossary at the back of this book there is also a list of useful words used in science and their definitions.

Good luck!

We are a collection of cells

Did you know...?
Most cells are tiny but some are huge. An ostrich egg is a single cell that would make omelettes for a dozen people!

Top tip
There are many types of cell in your body – all of them are specialists at the job they do.

Once they fuse together the sperm and egg make a single cell. This grows and divides to form a new person.

All living things are built up from cells. These are like miniature chemical plants – they produce and process all the chemicals that are vital for living things. Large animals and plants are collections of millions of cells. Your body is made up from millions of cells of many different types. Most cells are tiny and can only be seen under a microscope. Your skin is made up from cells that fit together like paving slabs.

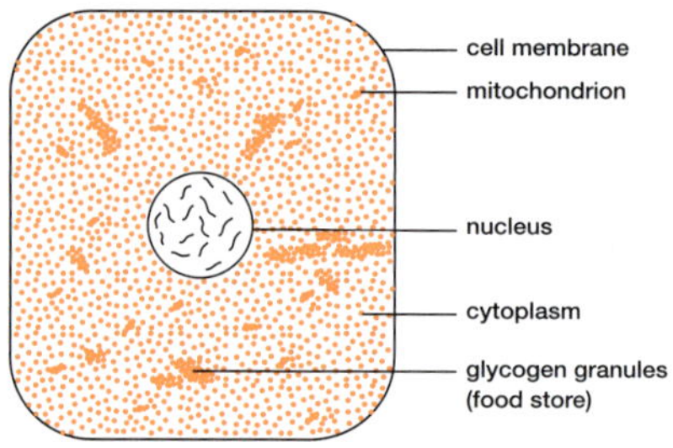

- ★ The cell membrane holds everything together.
- ★ The nucleus is the control centre of the cell.
- ★ Glycogen granules are the cell's food store.
- ★ Mitochondria are power packs for the cell.

Millions of these cells fit together to make sheets of skin.

Types of cell

As well as skin cells, there are many other types of cell in your body. Each type of cell has a particular job to do. The shape and makeup of each cell reflects what it does in the body.

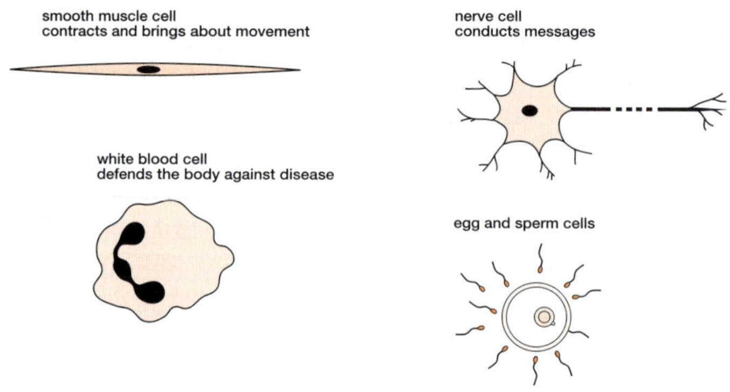

- ★ Smooth muscle cell
  These cells can lengthen or shorten. When you pull up your arm, all the muscle cells in your biceps are shortening.
- ★ Nerve cell
  Nerve cells are long and thin. They transmit messages.
- ★ White blood cell
  These attack microbes in your blood stream.
- ★ Sperm and egg cells
  Human eggs are much bigger than the sperm, but both are single cells.

Plant cells

As in animals there are a variety of plant cell types. The cells on the root, for instance, have special growths called root hairs that help to absorb water.

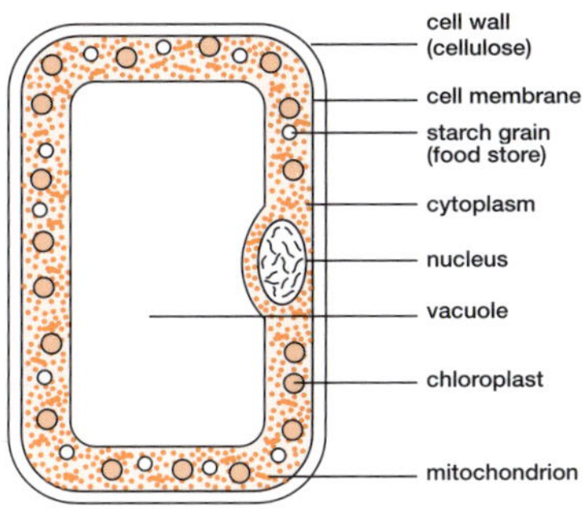

★ The cell wall is made of cellulose. This is what makes plants stiff enough to stand up.

★ The chloroplasts are green and help in photosynthesis.

★ Plant cells have a sap-filled space called a vacuole.

★ Starch grains form a food store

This is a plant cell from a leaf.

Plant and animal cells have several differences:

★ Plant cells have a cell wall. Animal cells only have a cell membrane.

★ Plant cells contain chloroplasts, which absorb the Sun's energy to provide food for the plant. Animal cells do not have chloroplasts.

★ Animal cells have small vacuoles.

Single celled organisms

Some plants and animals are made from only one cell. Amoeba are single-celled animals that live in damp places. They move by sliding out part of their body. Attach the labels below to the correct part of this drawing of an amoeba.

nucleus	cytoplasm	cell membrane

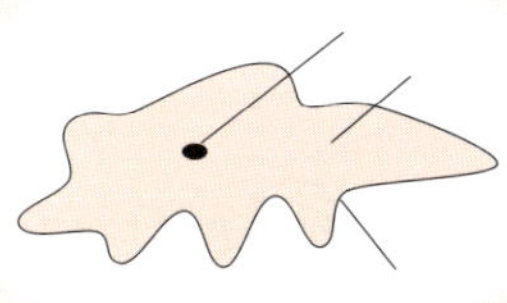

Activity

Pick up a leaf and feel the way that is stiff and crunchy. Compare this with your ear lobe, which is soft and squishy. This difference between plant and animal cells is due to the stiffness of the cell walls in plants.

What's the difference?

Plant cells differ from animal cells in a number of ways. Plant cells have:

★ a tough cell wall

★ a vacuole

★ chloroplasts

★ starch grains as a food store instead of glycogen

What happens when cells die?

When old cells die, new cells are formed by the old ones dividing into two. A baby starts as a single cell that divides and divides until it is a fully formed human with millions of cells.

An organism is a living thing.

Tissue and organs

Types of tissue

Some types of tissue can be found in many parts of the body. **Connective tissue** holds joints together in the form of ligaments. It acts as a cushion between bones in the form of **cartilage**. The tendons that join muscles to bones are also made of connective tissue.

The gut is lined with **epithelial cells**. These are covered with **muscle tissue** to make it possible to squeeze food down the tube.

Nerve tissue is found all over the body. It is quite fragile and is often protected by bone. The backbone has a long nerve, the **spinal cord**, running up the middle. If this is broken in an accident the injured person cannot use their legs.

Your body is made up from material called tissue. Body tissues are made from groups of similar cells.

There are many types of tissue in your body

- ★ Muscle tissue pulls your skeleton to enable you to move.
- ★ Epithelial tissue is the name given to sheets of tissue that form the skin.
- ★ Skeletal tissue is hard material that forms bones.
- ★ Connective tissue makes up the tough fibres that hold bones and other body parts together.
- ★ Nerve tissue is a network of cells with many connections

The stomach is a muscular bag lined with epithelial tissues. It is made from two types of cell. Epithelial cells form an inner tube of sheet tissue. Muscle cells form an outer bag to hold in the food. The muscles contract to help break down the food.

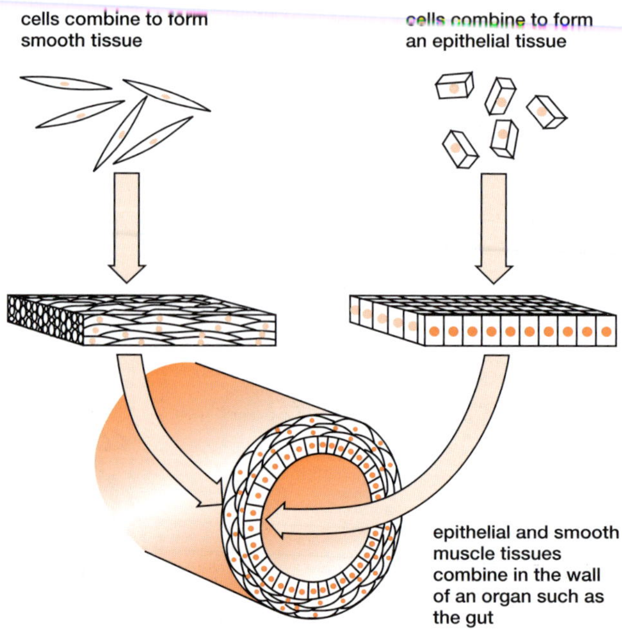

The stomach lining is made from tissue like skin and the bag is made from muscles, which can contract and stretch.

What's inside?

There are many different organs in your body. All organs are made from tissue. Match the labels to the correct body part.

heart

brain

intestines

stomach

lungs

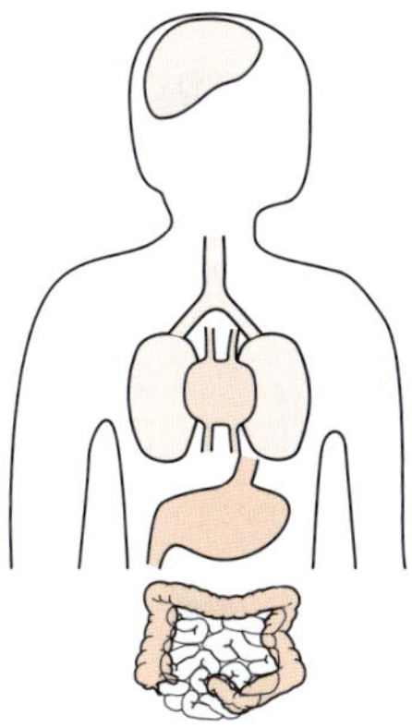

Match the description to the pictures.

Heart squeezes once per second to pump blood along. It is made mainly from muscle tissue.

Brain is made mainly from nerve tissue.

Lungs are bags that take in fresh air and push out used gases.

Gut is a tube down which food passes.

Stomach is a bag that starts to digest food.

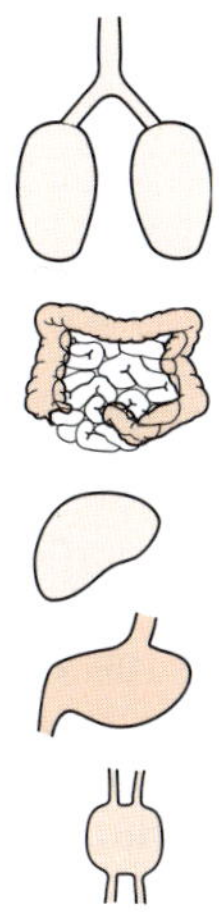

Mend the injury

When you injure your body or get a disease, certain types of tissue are affected. Write in the tissue affected in each of these diseases or injuries. The first is done for you.

Injury or disease	Type of tissue
Twisted ankle (Pain in a joint)	Connective tissue
Sunburn	______________
Heart attack (Pain in the heart)	______________
Broken leg	______________
Alzheimer's (Difficulty remembering)	______________

Did you know...?

All these tissues can re-grow. Look at the way that your skin covers a cut in a few days. Doctors are trying to make nerve cells grow and join themselves up again in spinal cord injuries.

Try it yourself

In the butchers, look for different types of animal tissue. Heart and steak are both muscle. Brain is rarely eaten these days but is soft. Liver is full of blood and is very good for health.

In some traditional butchers the lining of the gut is used to make long thin sausages. Haggis is made by stuffing a sheep's stomach.

Reproduction and growing up

The main sex hormones are the female hormone **oestrogen** and the male hormone **testosterone**.

Did you know...?

In medieval times some boy singers had their testicles removed. This prevented puberty and their voices stayed high like a woman's.

Ovum is the singular for an egg cell. Ova is the plural for egg cells.

It is not known why the month from new moon to new moon (see page 53) is the same length as the menstrual cycle.

Many women feel tense and irritable at some point in their menstrual cycle.

Puberty happens for most people between the ages of 12 and 14. It happens in girls slightly earlier than boys. Puberty is caused by sex hormones, which bring on many changes in children's bodies.

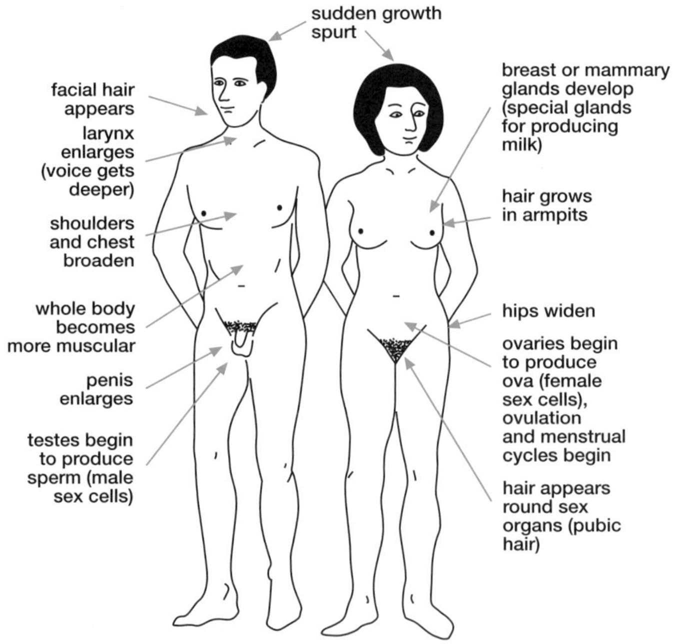

Many changes happen during puberty.

male	both	female
★ The voice becomes lower. ★ Hair grows on the face. ★ The testicles begin to produce sperm.	★ Hair grows under the arms and between the legs ★ Sudden growth in height.	★ The breasts begin to swell. ★ Menstruation produces monthly bleeding from the vagina.

Sexual parts

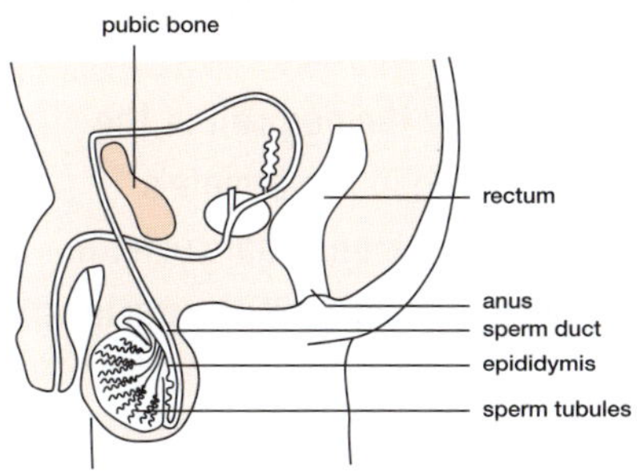

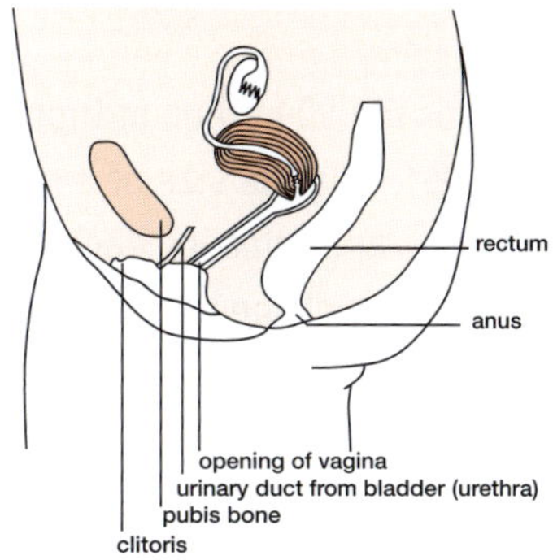

Menstrual cycle

Menstruation is a monthly cycle.

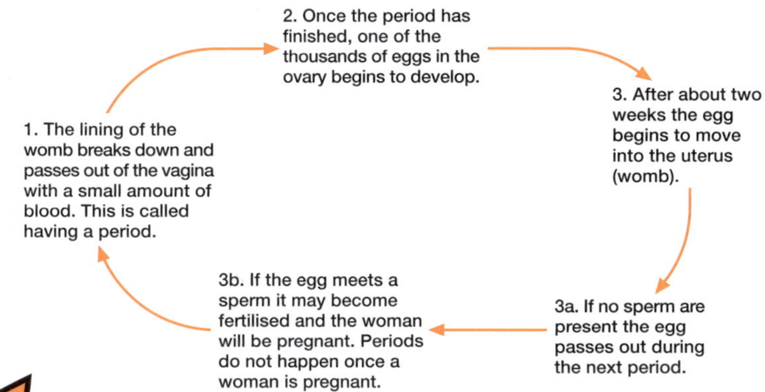

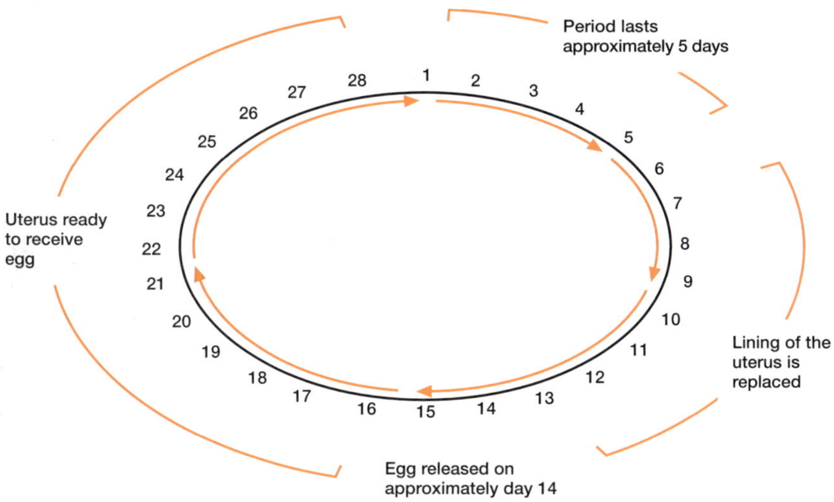

In the Arctic

Polar bears mate in the autumn so that their cubs are born early in spring when the female can hunt most easily.

Activity

Find out about the breeding seasons of different animals.

Why do you think the spring is a good time to have young?

Growth of a baby

Once it has been fertilised, the egg cell divides and increases in size. At that point it is called an **embryo**.

Once the fertilised cells reach approximately seven weeks old it looks like a person and is called a **foetus**.

Fertilisation

Out of the 50 million million cells in the human body the egg cell is the largest. It is the size of a pin head. Ova are produced in the female's ovaries and released each month in the middle of the menstrual cycle. In the centre of the ovum there is a nucleus. The sperm's head is the nucleus of the sperm cell.
Fertilisation of the egg happens if a sperm joins with the egg.

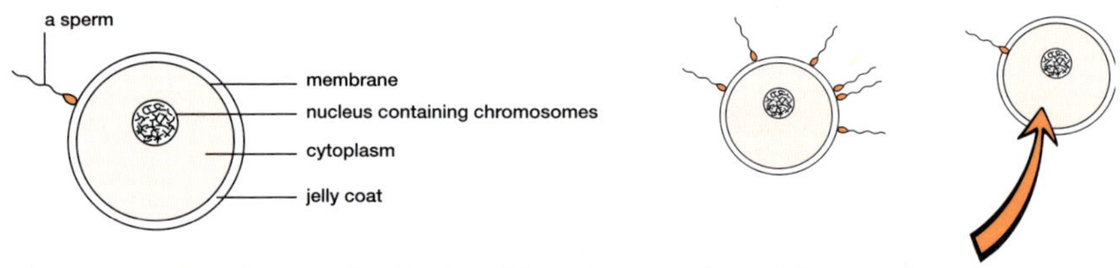

Once one sperm has pushed its head into the covering of the egg the other sperm cannot get in.

Foetal development

After it has been fertilised the egg attaches itself to the lining of the uterus. It develops there for approximately 270 days. In that time it is supplied with food and oxygen from its mother by the umbilical cord and the placenta.

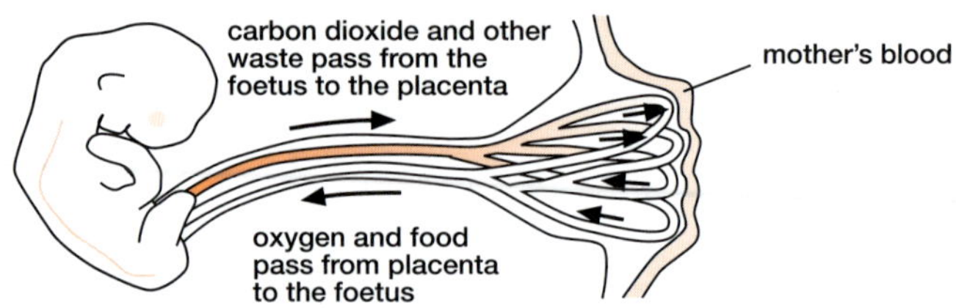

The baby is supplied with all it needs by its mother. All the waste products from the baby, such as carbon dioxide, pass out into the mother's body.

The baby in the uterus lives in a pond of water called amniotic fluid. This tells you that the baby cannot be breathing air through its mouth. The amniotic fluid protects the baby from being damaged if its mother bumps into things.

The placenta

The human embryo grows in the mother's uterus. It is supplied with food and oxygen from the mother's blood. The two do not actually mingle but food and oxygen pass into the baby through the placenta.
Although many harmful things **cannot** pass between mother and baby, some drugs such as nicotine, alcohol and painkillers **can** cross from the mother to baby. Many germs are prevented from passing through the placenta but some, such as syphilis bacteria, are able to go through.

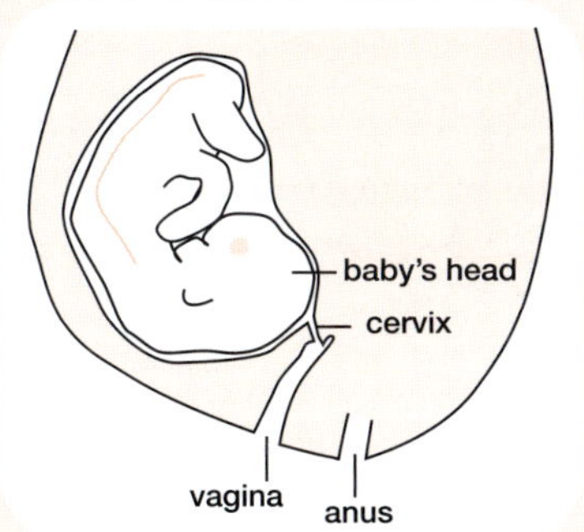

Growth rates

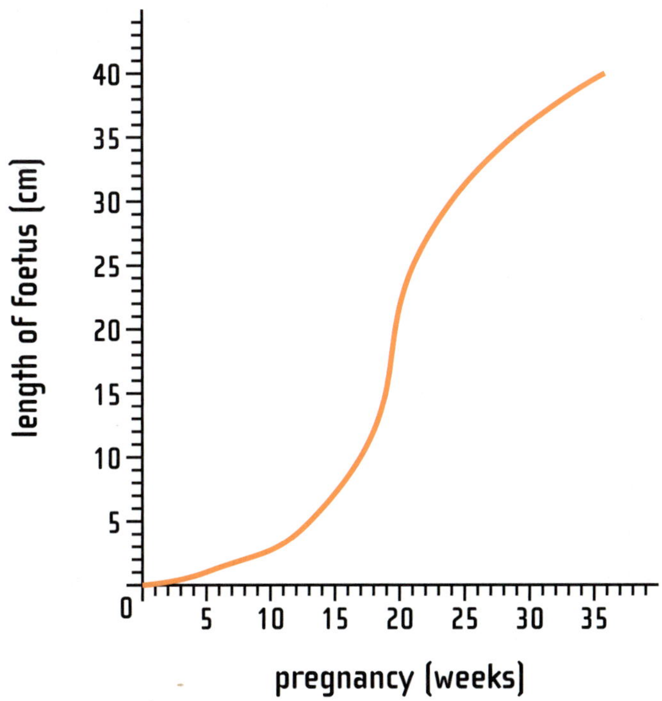

A human embryo starts as bundles of cells. It grows extremely rapidly at first.

Big baby!

Humans keep their babies inside until they are very big. Babies' brains are very large and well-developed compared with the rest of their bodies.

I need my mummy!

Many babies are dependent on their parents for a time after they are born. Blue whales stay with mother for three years after they are born. Elephants stay with mother for five years. Why do you think humans need to spend so long with their parents?

Plant reproduction

Did you know...?

The biggest flowers in the world are one metre across and grow on the Rafflesia plant in the jungles of south east Asia. The flowers look and smell like rotting meat. They attract flies that want to lay their eggs on decaying flesh. These flies **pollinate** the flowers.

Birds and bees

In Britain most flowers are pollinated by bees. This is not true in all parts of the world. In South America many flowers are pollinated by humming birds. In all cases, the insects or birds come to the flower to drink nectar.

Flower structure

Flowers are the plant's way of making seeds. Most flowers contain male and female parts.

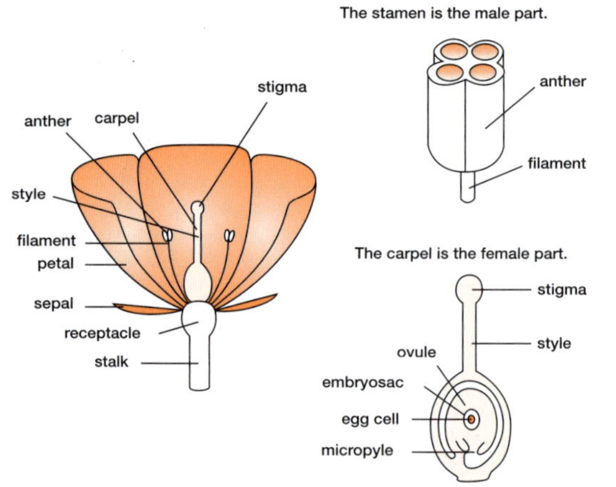

The male parts of a flower produce pollen. This is the flower equivalent of sperm. Pollen is made in anthers held on the end of slender filaments. Female parts produce the seeds, which are fertilised by the male pollen. The stigma is at the top of the female parts. It is connected by the style to the ovary. The ovary is full of ovules. These are the equivalent of eggs in a female animal.

Flowers come in all shapes and sizes. Label these diagrams of different flowers:

anther	filament	stigma	style	ovary

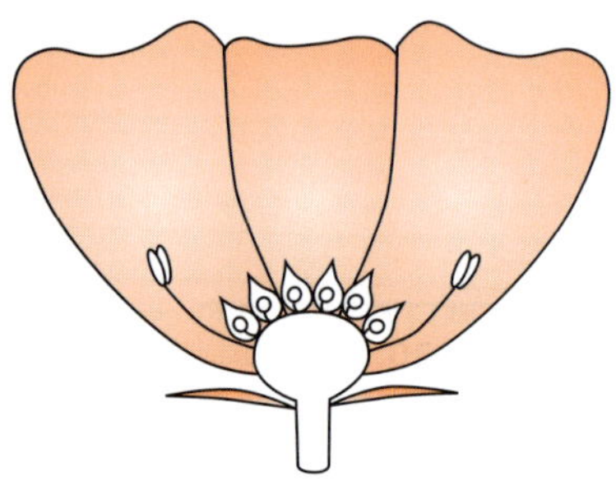

buttercup

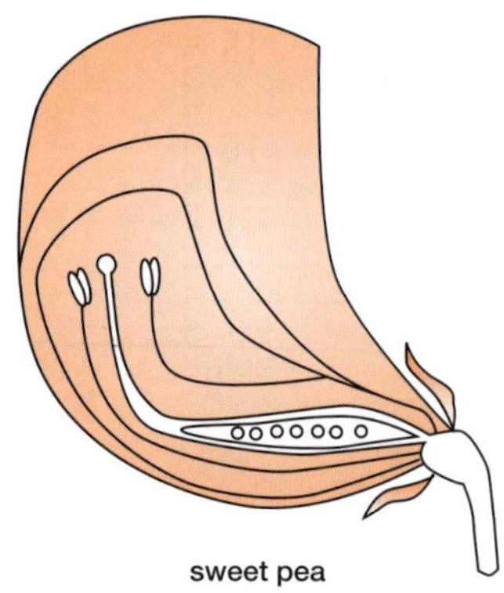

sweet pea

Fertilisation

Once the male pollen reaches the female ovule they join together to make a seed. Inside a seed there is an embryo plant.

Try it yourself

Look for seeds in your food cupboard or buy some dried peas and beans from the supermarket. Soak them for a couple of hours. The seed coat has a tiny hole that allows water and air into the seed.

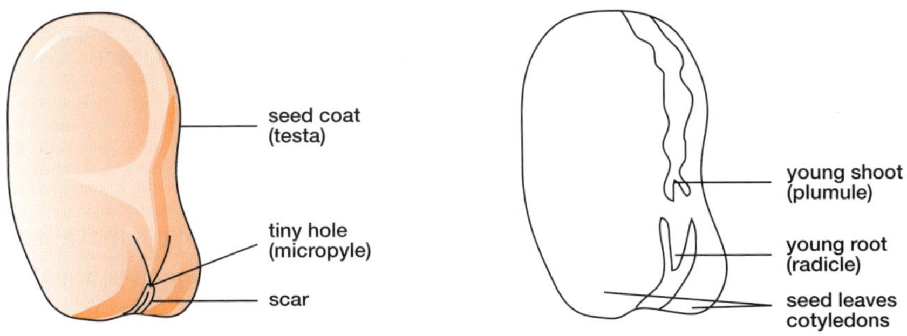

Slide off the seed coat and try to spot the young shoot and root. Plant the soaked seed in a pot of soil, compost, wool or string (anything really) and look at the way in which the shoot and root grow.

Seed dispersal

Seeds are spread in many different ways.

- Wind blows dandelion and sycamore.
- Animals spread acorns when making a food store.
- Seeds with hooks get a ride on furry animals.
- Holly berries pass through birds and grow where they are dropped.

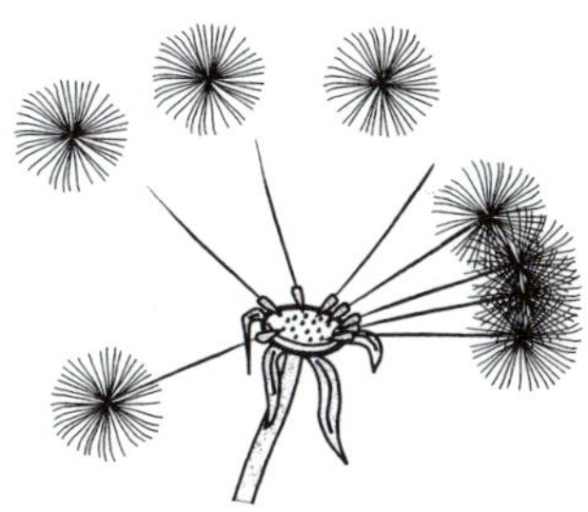

Dandelion

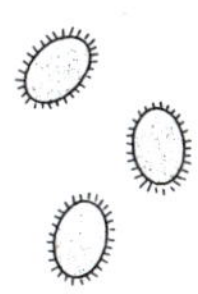

Burdock burrs

Only pollen from the same species of plant will fertilise the ovules of a flower. If the plant fertilises its own ovules this is called **self-fertilisation**.

Environment

Energy from the Sun

Green plants are the only living things that can make food. They do this using the energy of the Sun. We call green plants producers. Animals cannot make their own food and have to eat plants or other animals. Animals are consumers.

Food chains

On the grasslands of East Africa grass is eaten by zebras. These are in turn eaten by lions. This is a short food chain.

grass → zebra → lion

A longer food chain can be traced in the Antarctic where tiny plants called phytoplankton are eaten by shrimps called krill. These are eaten by small fish which are in turn eaten by penguins. Some penguins are eaten by killer whales. There is nothing large enough or fierce enough to eat a killer whale making it the top predator in the chain.

phytoplankton → krill → fish → penguin → killer whale

People and food chains

People are the end consumers in many food chains. In a meal like this one you can trace the links in the chain.

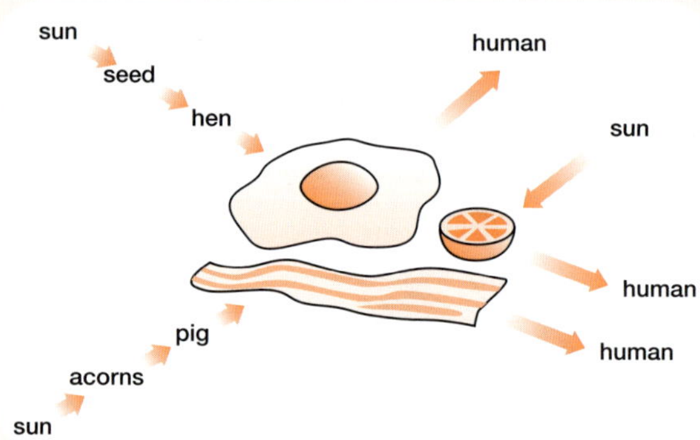

If a person ate the zebra and was then caught and eaten by a lion the food chain would have one more link.

We must be careful!

In the 1990s some people caught a disease from eating meat from cows that had been given food made from other dead animals. We need to know how our food has been produced.

Pyramid of numbers

In each of the food chains we have looked at there are fewer animals at each level. For instance, there are many more zebras than lions. There are many more fish than penguins. In any food chain not all the energy is passed up to the next level. Some of the energy is used by the animals as they move around.

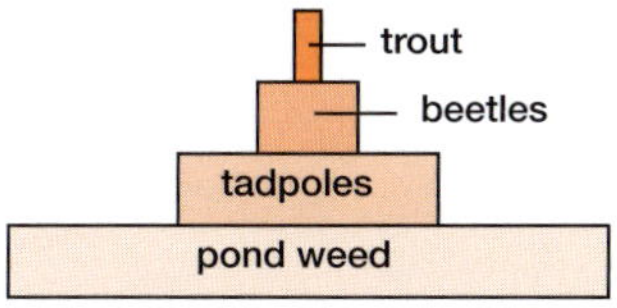

The number of living things at each level decreases. This pyramid of numbers also reminds us that the total mass of living things at each level is also less.

Food webs

All the animals and plants in an environment are linked in a food web. This diagram shows the way in which animals in a pond are linked in a food web. If one part of the food web dies out, all the rest of the animals in the web are affected. For instance, if all the animals that ate tadpoles were removed from the pond, there would be many more tadpoles but fewer top predators, like pike.

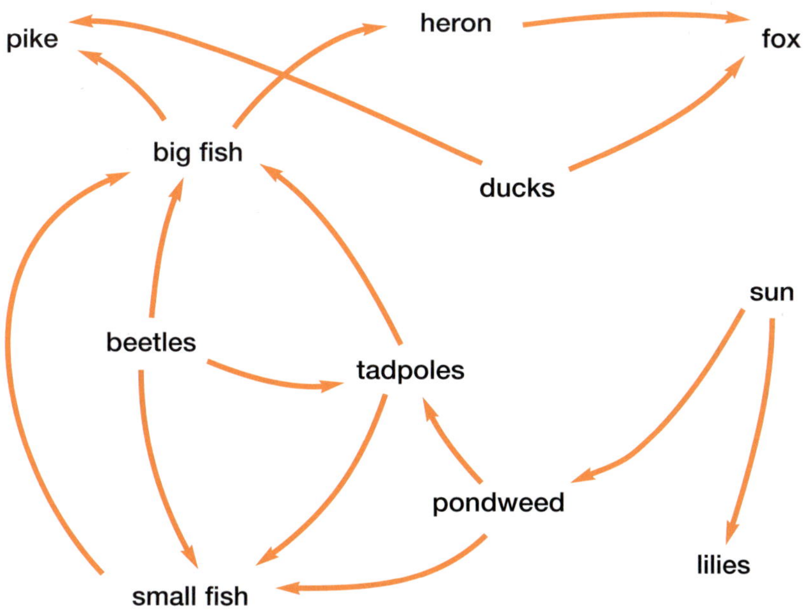

There are fewer of each animal up the food chain and the total mass is less.

Activity

Make a vivarium in an old aquarium. A vivarium is a container of living things. Cut a turf of grass and some soil. Watch what grows in your soil and turf. If you can find slugs and snails add these and feed them on lettuce or apple slices.

Animals with backbones

Many types of fish have **swim bladders**, which they use to help keep them floating below the surface of the water. Sharks do not have a swim bladder and will sink if they do not swim at all times.

The skin of some types of tree frog is very poisonous. People who live in the South American jungles use the mucus from the frog's skin to tip their blow darts.

The dinosaurs are an extinct group of reptiles.

Backbones

The bones that run down your back from neck to bottom are the spine or vertebral column. It is made from a series of bones stacked on top of each other. All animals that have a spine are called vertebrates. There are five main types of vertebrate animals.

Fish

Fish live in water and breathe through gills. Their bodies are covered with scales, which protect the skin and stop water going through the fish's skin. Fish come in all shapes and sizes, ranging from sharks to seahorses. Fish have rows of teeth, which are replaced as they are worn out.

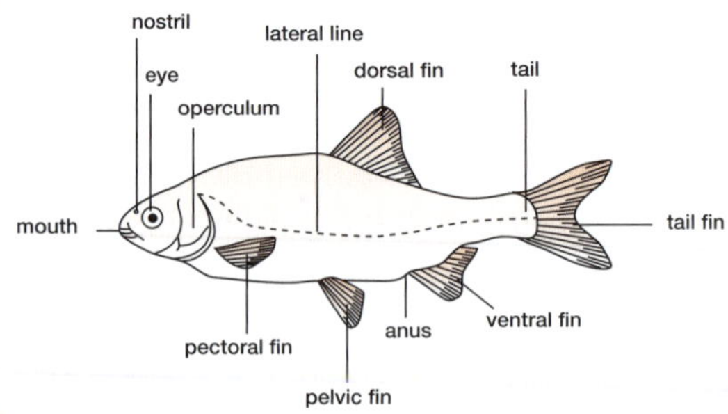

Amphibians

This group of vertebrates includes frogs, toads and newts. The skin of amphibians is moist and usually rather slippery. This means that amphibians have to live in damp places. They are cold-blooded animals.

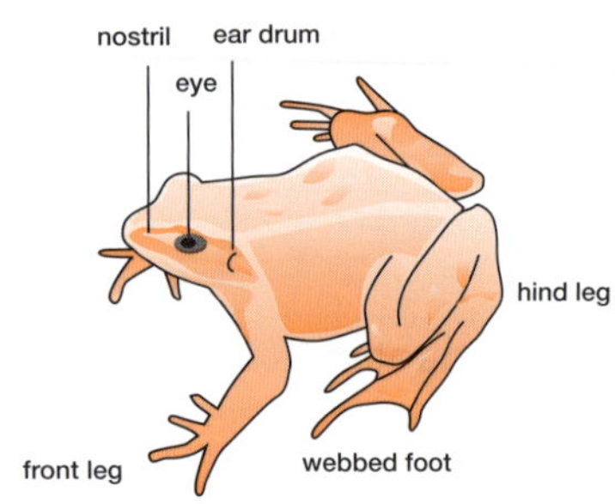

Reptiles

Lizards, snakes and crocodiles are reptiles. Their skin is dry and scaly and this means they can live in hot dry parts of the world. Unlike amphibians, which have to lay their eggs in water, reptiles lay leathery eggs on land.

Birds

If an animal has feathers it must be a bird. The arms of birds have evolved into wings and all birds have a beak. There is a wide range of adaptation of the beak and feet. For instance, ducks have flat beaks and webbed feet to help them swim, while ospreys have a sharp hooked beak and talons for gripping prey.

Birds are warm-blooded animals and they have feathers to help keep them warm. Examine a feather in detail. Use a strong magnifier to look at the way the barbs hook together to make a sheet of feather. Put a drop of water on the feather and see if it is absorbed by the feather.

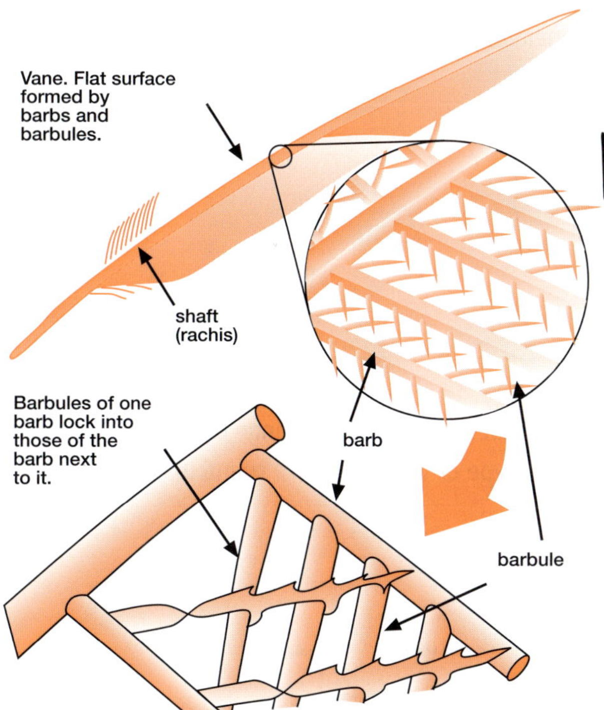

Mammals

We are mammals. Cats and dogs are mammals. The bodies of mammals are covered in hair. Humans have a thin covering compared with most other mammals. Mammals feed their young on milk, which is produced by the female from teats on the chest.

Mammals are very varied. A few mammals, such as seals, whales and dolphins, live in the sea. Bats are mammals that can fly.

Many scientists think that birds are the descendants of dinosaurs. Fossils of birds have reptile and bird features.

Birds vary in size from the ostrich, which is two metres tall, to a hummingbird, which is only 5 cm long.

Most mammals give birth to live young. The spiny anteater and the duck-billed platypus, both from Australia, do not.

Activity

Play this odd one out games. Which is the odd one out from:

- ★ dolphin, whale, shark
- ★ eagle, bat, swallow
- ★ snake, tortoise, frog
- ★ python, eel, turtle.

Make up some more odd ones out of your own.

Animals without backbones

This group of animals is called the coelenterates.

Did you know ...?

Many worms are parasitic. This means that they live on or inside other animals. The worms that cats and dogs have inside their intestines are a type of internal parasite.

External skeletons

The majority of animals that live on Earth do not have a bony skeleton in the body like humans. They are either soft, like a worm, or have a hard covering and soft insides. Think of a poor snail which you carelessly tread on – once the shell is broken the rest of the body is soft and easily squashed.

Animals without legs

Jellyfish and anemones have soft bodies with stinging tentacles.

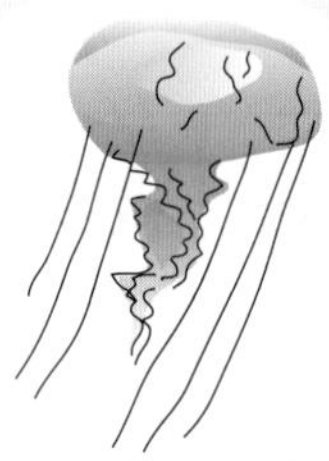

Worms are soft-bodied and come in a range of shapes and sizes. Earthworms are a type of worm that are round in cross section. Leeches are flatter.

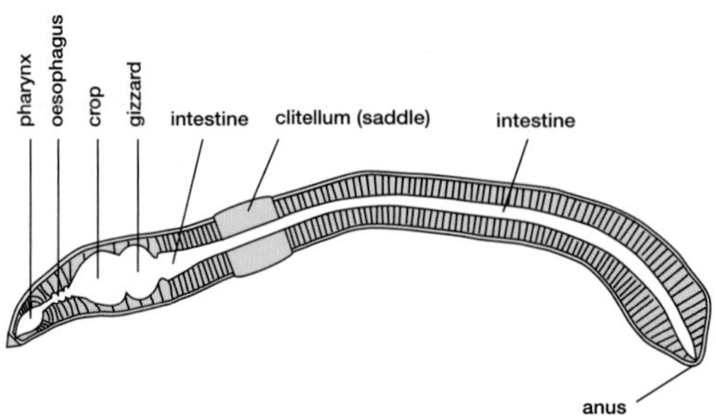

Snails, slugs, shellfish and octopus are all molluscs. Most of these have a shell but in some cases it is so small, or inside the body, that it is difficult to see.

Animals with jointed legs

On the seashore you might pick up a crab. Its legs are jointed and it has a hard shell. Crabs are just one type of animal which does not have an internal skeleton but does have jointed legs. There are many millions of types of this kind of animal. They are called arthropods (arthro = joint, pod = foot or leg).

Crabs, lobsters and woodlice are all crustaceans. This group has at least eight legs and two pairs of feelers. They mainly live in water.

Centipedes and millipedes have many pairs of jointed legs. Their long thin bodies are divided into segments.

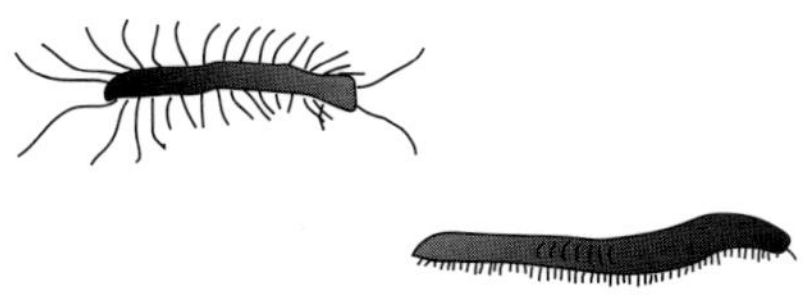

Spiders and scorpions have eight legs. They lack feelers and all live on land.

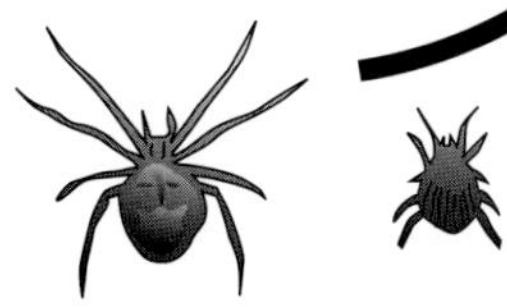

The biggest and most varied of the arthropods are the insects. All insects have six legs. The body is divided into three parts: head, thorax and abdomen. Insects include bees, wasps, ants, beetles, moths and butterflies.

Activity

If it is summer, try to find a dead wasp or bee or another type of insect. Look carefully at the body and see if you can see the three parts of the animal. Look at the place where the legs are joined to the body. Which section is this? Is it the same in all insects?

Woodlice can only live in damp conditions as they still breathe through gills hidden under their shell. They suffocate in dry air like fish.

This group is called the **arachnids**. It is named after a woman in Greek mythology who was a fantastic spinner of threads.

Amazing insects

Insects have a wonderful life cycle. Their bodies go through different stages, ranging from egg to **larva** to **pupa**. You may have studied the life cycle of a butterfly, which follows this pattern.

Fungi and green plants

Foot fungus!

Fungi can grow in damp places. This might include between your toes! Athlete's foot is caused by a fungus.

Take care if you do this with toadstools. Do not eat them (obviously!) and be aware that many toadstools contain hundreds of maggots that will come crawling out in the warmth of your room!

Giant algae occur in the form of kelp, which can grow strands hundreds of metres long.

Fungus

Toadstools, mushrooms and mould are all types of fungus. Fungi differ from green plants in that they cannot make their own food from sunlight. They feed by breaking down dead plant or animal material.

You can grow fungus safely on some old bread sealed in jam jars. Label the jars with the conditions you have in each of them. You might try these different conditions:

- damp old bread
- old bread lightly toasted before sealing the jar
- old bread sprinkled with sugar
- new bread straight out of the packet

Bread often grows a green mould called Penicillium from which the antibiotic penicillin is extracted. So you can see that mould is very useful to us. Once mould begins to grow look at the shape of the mould. Does the mould grow more quickly if the jar is kept in a warm or cool place?

Spore production

Take a large open mushroom or toadstool. Place it on a piece of black paper and leave for a few days. Once you remove the mushroom you will be left with a print of the spores that have fallen from the mushroom gills.

Spores are reproductive cells, similar in some ways to seeds in flowering plants.

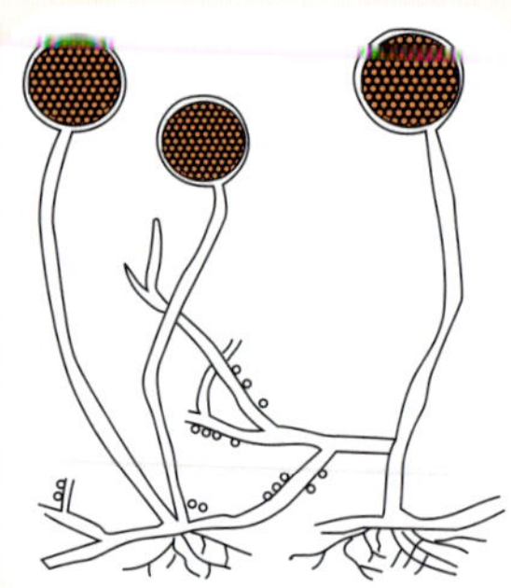

Algae

When you look into rock pools at the seaside all the plants you see in the pool are algae. These seaweeds include the green slime, which makes the rocks so slippery, as well as the beautiful red and green plants of the pools. Alga also occurs in ponds in the form of the green slime that builds up in summer.

One type of alga, which you will probably study, is called spirogyra. This alga is in the form of long thin strands called filaments. Each filament is merely a chain of cells. The slime that makes spirogyra so slippery prevents the long thin filaments from getting tangled.

Lichens

The crusty looking yellow, grey or green growths that occur on stones or tree trunks are likely to be lichen. These plants can grow in very extreme conditions where no other plants can possibly grow. They survive with hardly any water and can stand great extremes of temperature. They grow very slowly indeed. Amazingly these plants are combinations of two living things: an alga and a fungus.

Mosses

On top of walls you will often see miniature forests of ferny green plants. These miniature green plants are likely to be mosses. They can grow in very little soil and with little water. Mosses do not produce seeds. Instead they reproduce using spores, which are spread from the capsules at the tips of the stalks.

Activity

Make a tiny moss and plant garden on a plate from moss you carefully remove from walls. Try not to take too much from any one place and try to make a collection of several different types of moss.

Symbiosis

In lichen the fungus forms the framework for the plant to grow and the alga makes the food from sunlight. When two living things benefit each other it is called **symbiosis**.

Moss is the main plant that forms peat bogs. As the moss dies it is buried by new plants, but the old moss does not decay. This is because of the waterlogged and acid conditions, which prevent the fungi from living on the dead moss.

Classifying materials

Molecules are made from groups of atoms.

That makes scents!

Have you ever wondered how you can smell perfume? It changes to a gas when warmed on a person's skin and the particles of gas move through the air. Some molecules of the perfume reach your nose.

Lard and wax

Lard and wax both become clear when melted but they are not see-through when solid. This is because they partly crystallise as they cool.

Did you know...?

At home you will almost certainly have some tungsten, which has a very high melting point (3410 °C). It is used to make the filaments in most light bulbs because it will not melt even when extremely hot.

Rock melts at about 1200 °C in a volcano.

Atoms and molecules

All materials are made up from particles. We call these particles atoms and molecules. In solids the particles are in fixed positions and do not move around much. In liquids the particles are still close together but they can slide past each other. In a gas the atoms and molecules are spread out and move around rapidly.

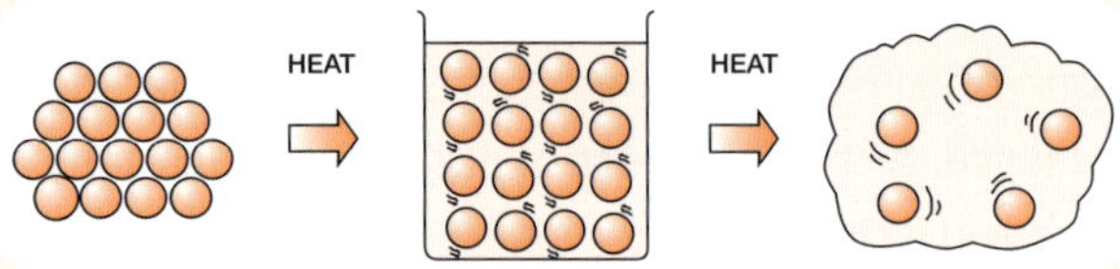

Heating

When materials are heated the particles that make up the material move around more. When a solid changes to a liquid the atoms and molecules can slide past each other allowing the liquid to flow. If a liquid is heated so it changes into a gas, the particles begin to move around so fast that they lose contact with each other. In a gas there is no attraction between the molecules and atoms.

In a candle you can see the three states of matter.

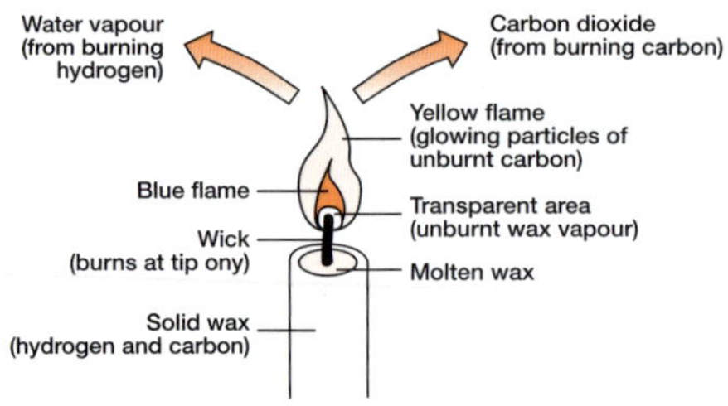

- The flame is where wax gas is burning
- The pool of wax near the wick is liquid wax.
- The candle is solid wax.

Melting point and boiling point

Water freezes at 0 °C and boils at 100 °C. Each material melts and boils at particular temperatures.

Iron melts at 1535 °C boils at 3000 °C	**Mercury** melts at minus 40 °C boils at 357 °C	**Lead** melts at 327 °C boils at 1744 °C

Is it really solid?

Powders, such as flour, can imitate some of the characteristics of liquids. They can flow and their surfaces are nearly level. Look at one grain though – it is obviously a solid.

Density

Just as each material has a special melting and boiling point, each material has a particular density. Density is the mass of one cubic centimetre of the material.

- 1 cm^3 of water has a mass of 1 gram.
- 1 cm^3 of iron has a mass of 8 grams.
- 1 cm^3 of silver has a mass of 11 grams.
- 1 cm^3 of gold has a mass of 19 grams.

Archimedes (the ancient Greek who jumped out of his bath shouting Eureka!) knew the density of gold. He caught out a jeweller who was making the king's crown out of metal that looked like gold but did not have gold's density.

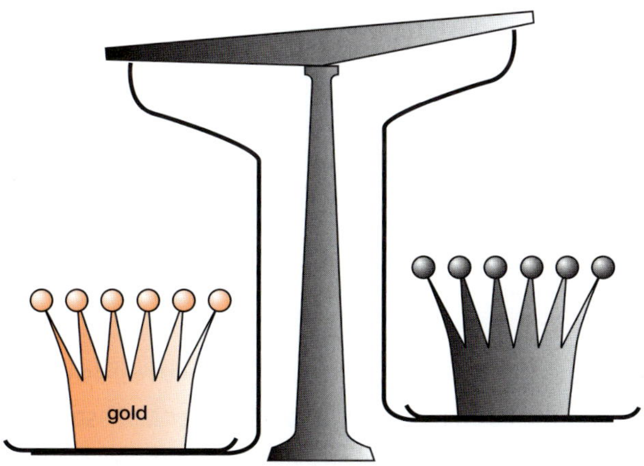

If the crowns are identical in shape and size, the one made out of gold will be heavier than the one made from a mixture of gold and copper.

Which weighs more?

One kilogram of lead and one kilogram of feathers weigh the same but the volume of feathers is much greater than that of lead.

Activity

Make a collection of different metals. Which ones feel heavy for their size and which feel light for their size?

Evaporating, condensing and dissolving

A volume of a solvent has a certain number of spaces to dissolve a solid. You might think of it like seats in a grandstand – as it gets fuller it is more and more difficult to get a seat.

Dissolving

When a solid dissolves in water it forms a solution. You can tell when a solution has been formed because you can see through the solution and the dissolved solid does not settle on the bottom.
In a solution, the particles of solvent and solute are evenly dispersed.

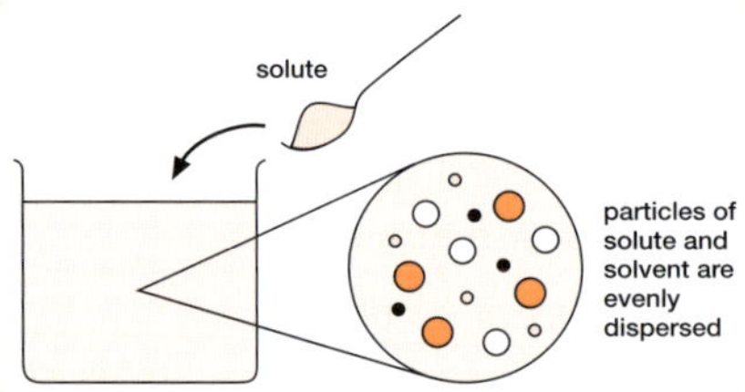

When you make a solution the mass of the solution is the same as the mass of the liquid and the solid added together.

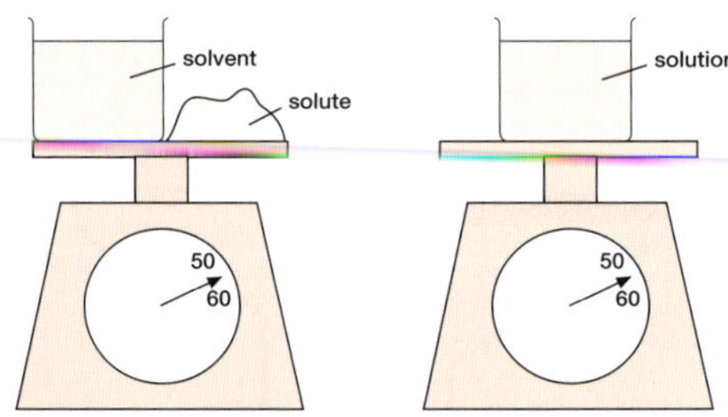

Saturation

Have you noticed that the first spoon of sugar is easy to dissolve in a small cup of water but as you keep adding sugar it takes longer to dissolve? Eventually the solution becomes saturated and no more sugar can be dissolved.

Solubility in warm and cold water

It is easier to dissolve sugar in warm water than it is in cold water. Try it for yourself! This means that it takes more sugar to saturate warm water than cold water. This is not true for all materials. Common salt (sodium chloride – NaCl) does not become easier to dissolve in warm water.

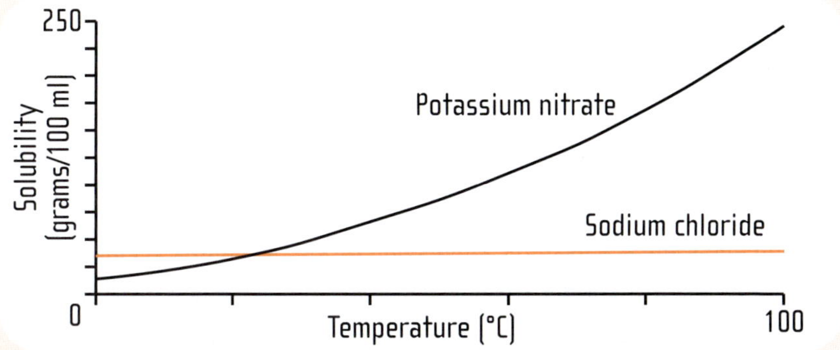

Gases dissolve

Carbon dioxide dissolves in water to make drinks fizzy. If the drink is warm, the carbon dioxide bubbles out very quickly. If the drink is cold, the carbon dioxide stays in solution.

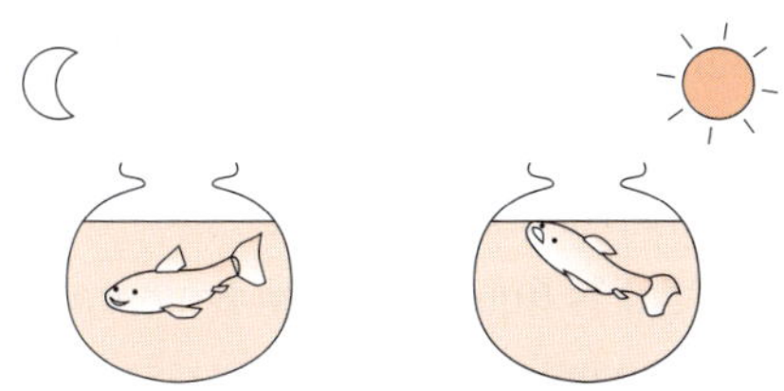

Oxygen dissolves better in cold water than in warm water. In warm water fish come to the surface to get more air.

Different solvents

Oily and greasy solids do not dissolve in water. Material like gloss paint will dissolve in paraffin or white spirit.

Mixtures that look like solutions

- An emulsion is a mixture of tiny particles of one liquid spread in another liquid, for example oil and vinegar salad dressing.
- A colloid is a mixture where solids are broken up into such tiny pieces that it does not settle and cannot be filtered. Milk is a colloid of water and tiny pieces of fat.

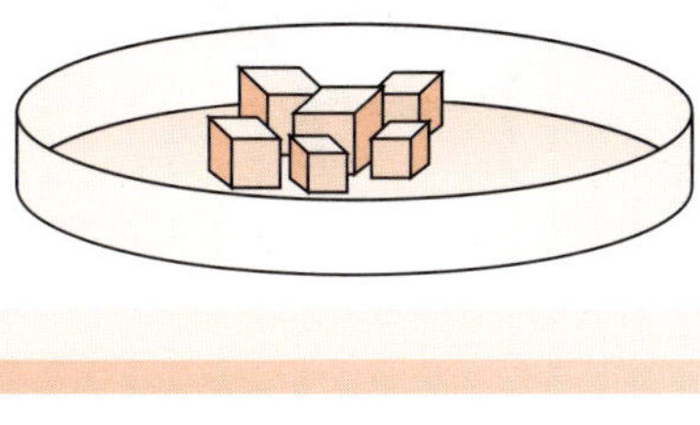

You can see from the graph that much more potassium nitrate dissolves as the temperature of the water rises.

Dry cleaners use a variety of different solvents to remove dirt from clothes. The one they don't use is water. That is why they are called DRY cleaners!

Activity

Dissolve some salt in water. Leave the solution on a saucer to evaporate slowly. The crystals left as the water evaporates are beautiful cubes. Try to grow them even larger by allowing the water to evaporate very slowly.

Metals

Where do metals come from?

Metals are found mixed with rock as ores.

Aluminium is the commonest metal on Earth. However, it is quite difficult to extract from bauxite which is the commonest ore of aluminium.

While all metals conduct electricity, some do it better than others. Gold and silver are very good conductors but they are too expensive to make wires.

Common metals

We use metals for many purposes.

- Iron and steel are used for knives and forks, car bodies, fridges, nails, screws and many other items which need to be strong but cheap.
- Aluminium is a light, shiny metal that we use for drinks cans and foil in the kitchen. It is used for power lines as it is light and strong.
- Copper is a red-brown metal, which is quite soft but tough. We use it in electrical wires and water pipes. Copper is mixed with gold to make jewellery that is cheaper than pure gold.
- Gold is a heavy metal prized for its beauty and resistance to change. It conducts electricity really well and is used in expensive electrical switches.
- Lead is a heavy metal that has a low melting point (see page 24). It was used for pipes in Roman times. It is now used to protect people who work in hospitals from harmful x-rays.
- Mercury is a metal that is liquid at room temperature. It is used in thermometers as it expands as the temperature rises.

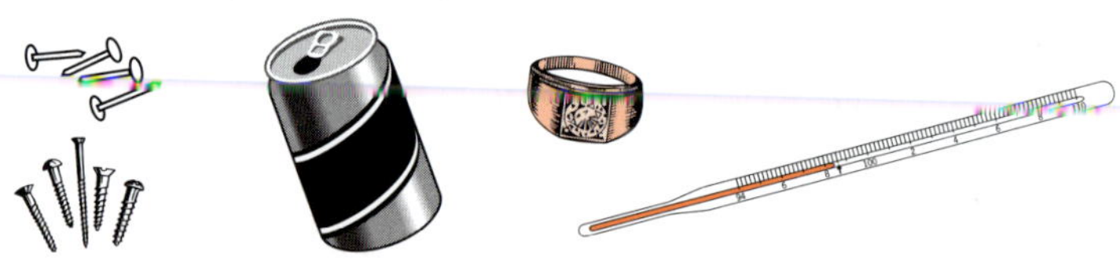

Properties of metals

- All metals are fairly dense.
- They make a ringing sound when struck.
- They conduct electricity.
- They conduct heat quite well.
- Iron, steel, cobalt and nickel are all attracted to magnets. The other metals are not.

Metal changes

If you leave an iron object outside, it is likely to rust. You can prevent rust forming by painting the iron or coating it with oil. This stops the water and air reaching the metal. Rust is iron oxide.

This list shows the chemical symbol of some metals. The metals at the top of the list change most easily when there is water present.

Metal	Chemical symbols
potassium	K
sodium	Na
calcium	Ca
magnesium	Mg
aluminium	Al
zinc	Zn
iron	Fe
lead	Pb
copper	Cu
gold	Ag

You may be puzzled looking at the list – aluminium does not change much if left in the rain. That is because it reacts quickly with air and water to form a thin layer, which protects the metal below the altered layer.

Using metals

Which metal would you use for the following jobs? Look at the properties of metals on the opposite page.

1. Girders for large buildings ____________________
2. Expensive coating for wrist watches ____________________
3. Making a racing bike ____________________

Why would you definitely not use these?

1. Mercury for making wires ____________________
2. Iron for making jewellery ____________________
3. Aluminium for fishing line weights ____________________

Stainless steel

To make stainless steel, the metal chromium is added. This prevents rusting and the metal stays shiny and smooth.

Activity

Try to get hold of a magnet. Test the metals in your home to see which are steel and iron and which are neither. Test 1p and 2p coins. Some will be magnetic, while others will not! Look at the dates and try to spot the pattern. Test cans to see which are steel and which are aluminium.

Acids and bases

? **Did you know...?**

In the 18th century British sailors got a disease called **scurvy** because their shipboard diet lacked essential vitamins. The best source of these was limes. That is why the Americans occasionally call British people limeys to this day.

Never handle bleach or paint stripper.

Acids

Lemons and grapefruit have a sharp sour taste. This is because they contain citric acid. Other citrus fruits include oranges, limes and tangerines. There are many other types of acid, some of which are beneficial:

- The sharp taste of cheese (lactic acid)
- Vinegar (acetic acid)
- The sting of a nettle (methanoic acid)
- Foods like carrots contain acids (ascorbic acid)
- The bite of ants (formic acid)
- There is strong acid in your stomach. When you are sick the horrid taste and furry feeling on your teeth is due to this acid.
- Acid in a car battery will damage your skin (sulphuric acid)

Acid rain

When rain falls through the air it dissolves carbon dioxide. This makes rainfall slightly acidic. If there is pollution in the air in the form of sulphur dioxide, then the rain can become much more acidic. Acid rain is a real problem in cities as it decays buildings made of limestone.

Bases and alkalis

The chemical opposite of an acid is a base. A base that has been dissolved in water is an alkali.

- Indigestion remedies are bases – they help counter the effects of too much acid in your stomach.
- Baking powder is a base.
- Soap is a mild alkali.
- Cleaning liquids used in the kitchen are often bases as they contain ammonia.
- Bleach is a strong alkali, which is very dangerous.
- Paint strippers are often strong and dangerous alkalis.

The strength of an acid or alkali

The strength of acids or alkalis is measured in pH. This stands for the power of hydrogen – it is a measure of the amount of hydrogen in the solution.

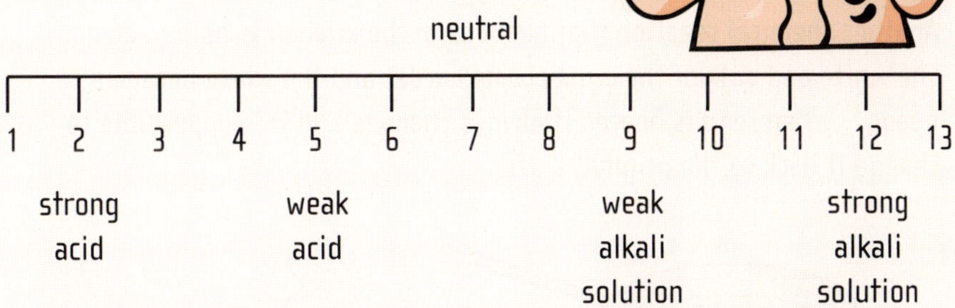

You would never taste chemicals to see if they were acid or base. Chemists use indicators to test whether solutions are acid or alkali. Indicators can also tell you how strong the acid or alkali is. Litmus paper turns red in an acid and blue in alkali.

Neutralising acids and bases

Acids and bases cancel each other out. When this happens, the solution becomes more neutral.

- **Antacids** If you have an upset stomach you might take an indigestion remedy. These remedies work by neutralising some of the acid in your stomach.
- **Wasp stings** Wasp stings are alkaline so some people say that dabbing a little vinegar on the sting might partly neutralise it.
- **Tooth decay** The build up of plaque on your teeth allows bacteria to live there. They are not directly responsible for tooth decay but they do produce acids that wear away the covering of your teeth. Mouthwashes have alkalis that neutralise these acids.
- **Soil acidity** Some soils are very acid and will not grow plants very well. Adding a base, such as lime, to the soil reduces the acidity of the soil.

Hydrogen

Hydrogen (chemical symbol H) is a very light gas. You are familiar with it as it is part of every flame you are likely to see in the home. It is also part of water – H_2O

Very strong antacids are used to help people with stomach ulcers. The acid in the stomach can wear away the lining of the stomach.

Chemical changes

Sweet fruit

Have you noticed that if you leave a greenish banana for a few days it goes yellow? It also tastes sweeter. The same thing happens with green tomatoes and plums. The reason the ripe fruit tastes sweeter is that a chemical reaction takes place in the fruit, which produces more sugar.

Opaque means that light cannot pass through it. **Transparent** is the opposite.

Heating food

Another chemical reaction that happens in the kitchen is boiling an egg. The white and yolk of the egg become harder and the white becomes opaque. When food is heated it always changes and it is impossible to change it back to the original state.

Heat causes chemical reactions in food. It is impossible to make the yolk and white runny again.

Most fruit will change in this way when cut. The process is called **oxidisation** as it is a change brought on by the gas oxygen (page 33).

Changes without heat

Leave a slice of apple in a dish. Notice that after a few hours it goes brown. This is due to a chemical reaction between the apple and the air. Experiment with some ways to slow down this reaction using equal sized pieces of cut apple.

- ★ Put one in the fridge
- ★ Put an acid (see page 30), such as lemon juice or vinegar, on the surface of the cut apple
- ★ Sprinkle a little sugar on the apple
- ★ Sprinkle a little salt on the apple
- ★ Cover it tightly with cling film

Which of these methods of slowing down a chemical change works best?

Burning things

When you burn a fuel, such as wax, wood, coal, gas or oil, it looks as if the fuel disappears as it is burnt. When fuels are burnt the atoms (page 24) of the fuel react with oxygen atoms from the air to make new chemicals.
In a car the petrol is burnt inside the engine. Carbon dioxide and water come out of the exhaust pipe. If you were to put all the exhaust gas into a huge balloon it would weigh more than the fuel that was put into the car in the first place.

Burning is a reaction between the fuel and the oxygen in the air. Oxygen makes up about 21% of the air we breathe.

Gas has mass

Gases weigh less than liquids and solids but they still have mass. How else would a hot air balloon float?

Activity

Make a chemical reaction using baking powder and vinegar. Put a spoon of baking powder into a jam jar. Pour a little vinegar into the baking powder and watch it fizz. The chemical reaction is producing a new solid and carbon dioxide.
With an adult helper, put a small candle in the jam jar before pouring in the vinegar. See what happens.

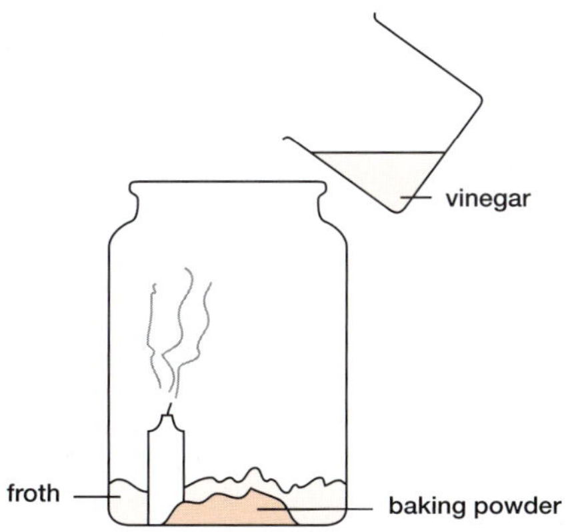

The carbon dioxide puts out the candle flame as oxygen cannot reach the flame.

Carbon dioxide

Many types of fire extinguisher use carbon dioxide to put out the flames.

Inside our own bodies there are many chemical reactions happening. One of these reactions makes us produce lots of carbon dioxide. Breathe into a jam jar and put it over a candle. Compare the length of time the flame stays alight with breathed out air and fresh air.

The air we breathe in contains only 0.004% carbon dioxide. The air we breathe out contains around 20%.

Energy resources

Did you know...?

Although hydrogen is burning in the Sun, there is no oxygen in space. The hydrogen is changing into helium under the great heat and pressure at its core. The Sun is using hydrogen fuel at an enormous rate. Luckily, there is enough hydrogen to last for billions of years.

Peat bogs

Nowadays, peat bogs are places where dead plants are forming thick layers. In parts of Russia this is being produced quite quickly, but in parts of England, where peat is being removed, none is replacing it. Peat can be burnt just like coal but is smoky and does not burn so well.

Another greenhouse gas is methane, which is produced by flatulence (farting) in cows!

The Sun

Our main energy supplies come from the Sun. It keeps us warm and its light allows plants to produce food (page 16). The Sun is a huge ball of burning hydrogen gas (page 31), which produces huge amounts of heat and light.
The temperature at the centre of the Sun is about 14 million degrees Celsius. At its surface it is only 6000 °C. Sunspots are areas where the surface temperature is lower than that.

Non-renewable energy

We get a lot of our energy from burning fuels, such as coal, gas and oil. All these are called fossil fuels because they were made millions of years ago and have remained buried in the ground until people came to dig them up. Coal was made by trees and mosses growing in swampy conditions nearly 250 million years ago. When these plants died they built up into thick layers as the water-logged swamps stopped them rotting away completely. These thick layers were buried by sands and muds and squashed. After many thousands of years the squashing turned the layers of dead wood and leaves into coal. The other fossil fuels, oil and gas, were produced from the bodies of long dead sea animals and plants. They too got their energy from sunlight. Once the supply of fossil fuels in the ground has been used up there will be no new supplies.
Burning fuels produces carbon dioxide (page 33). This is a greenhouse gas. Greenhouse gases are thought to be making the climate of the Earth change.

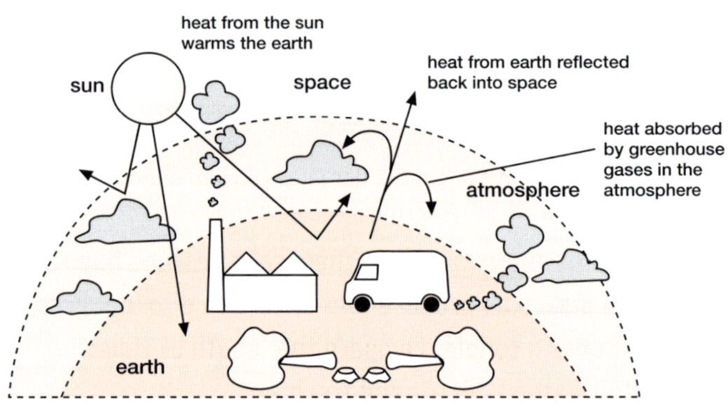

Gases such as carbon dioxide, methane and water vapour hold the heat from the Sun, stopping it from being lost into space.

Fossil fuel burning can also produce acid rain (see page 30). This happens when the gases from burning fuels are dissolved by the rain. Carbon dioxide produces the weak acid called carbonic acid. This acid is damaging limestone buildings in many parts of the world. The gases sulphur dioxide and sulphur trioxide are produced where sulphur is burnt. These gases can make sulphuric acid, which is strong enough to cause soil and lakes to become too acidic for animals and plants to live.

Renewable energy resources

Energy from the Sun is going to be arriving on the Earth for the next four billion years, so as far as people are concerned it will never run out. Sunlight can be used to produce electricity using photoelectric cells. People can use these as roof tiles in some countries to produce some of the electricity they need. Sunlight also provides the energy for plant growth. Fast growing trees can be harvested and burnt in power stations instead of using fossil fuels.

Heat from the Sun can be used to heat water, which we can use to heat our homes. Solar furnaces can concentrate the heat of the Sun. Small ones can heat food and huge ones can make water hot enough to drive electric generators.

The Sun's heat causes some parts of the Earth to be hotter than others (page 52) and this causes winds to blow. Wind turbines are good ways to turn an electricity generator in windy places.

Wind makes the waves form on the seas and oceans. If a generator is anchored in wavy seas the movement can be used to produce electricity. Tides in the seas change the levels of the sea four times a day. The huge movements of water can be used to drive generators in the dam walls.

Some people oppose this form of electrical generation, called hydroelectricity, because they think it will spoil the areas where it is located.

Sulphur is mixed in with coal and oil.

Desert power!

Enormous numbers of photoelectric cells could one day be put in desert areas and could produce huge amounts of electricity. The only problem is the length of the wires needed to get the electricity to where people live.

Wind turbines are simply propellers attached to a generator.

Hydroelectric power from damming rivers robs people of their homes and floods useful farmland.

Energy transfers

Heat energy

Molecules and atoms (page 24) are in constant motion. The more they move, the more heat energy they have. Heat is the transfer of energy from a hot object to a cooler one.

Most of the food we eat is turned into heat in our bodies.

Try it yourself

A person lifting 20 kg of shopping 50 cm into a car is doing 10 joules of **work**. Calculate all the work you do when helping adults with the weekly shop.

Energy in different forms

- Heat, light and electricity are forms of energy.
- Objects in motion have kinetic energy.
- Objects that have been raised off the ground have potential energy.

The weights have potential energy because they have been lifted off the ground.

- Chemical energy can be found in the form of food and fuels (page 34). This is a form of stored energy, which is changed into heat when food is digested in our bodies or when fuels are burnt.
- Strain energy is the form of energy stored in a stretched elastic band or a bow before it fires an arrow.

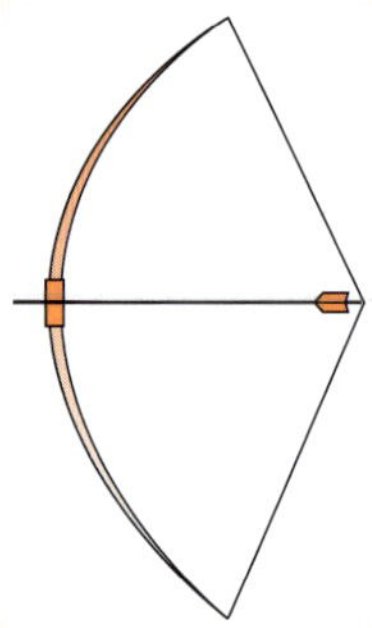

Measuring energy

Energy can do work. Work is measured in joules (J). Lifting a load of 10 kg one metre off the floor requires 10 J of work. One joule is defined as the work done moving a force of 1 newton a distance of one metre. See page 44 for the definition of a newton.

Energy changes

Energy cannot be created or destroyed but it can be changed in form. Pick up a small object from the table and then drop it on the floor. The object in your hand had energy of position (potential energy). Once you dropped it the object gained kinetic energy. Some of this was changed into sound energy as it hit the floor.

A cyclist at the top of a hill has potential energy but as she is not moving she has no kinetic energy. As she rolls down, all the potential energy is converted into kinetic energy.

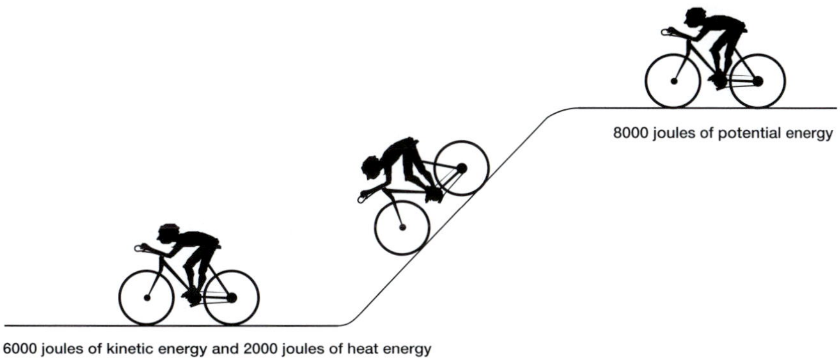

Some of the kinetic energy is converted into heat energy through friction on the tyres and bearings.

Efficiency of energy changes

- In a football match, players take in chemical energy in the form of food. They convert most of this into heat as they run around the pitch. Only a small part of their energy is used to work against air resistance and to kick the ball.

- An ordinary light bulb becomes very hot. This is wasted energy as we only want light from the bulb.

Activity

Stretch an elastic band from one finger. Ping it across the room. The chemical energy in the food you ate has been converted into strain energy in your muscles and the band. Once you let go, all that is converted into kinetic energy.

Where does the heat go?

All the energy changes we describe here end in heat. Heat does not disappear but it does get spread out in the environment and eventually is radiated out into space.

Working up a sweat!

We lose our heat energy by sweating. Changing sweat from liquid to gas requires heat energy from our bodies.

Energy saving lights

Efficient light bulbs and fluorescent tubes are much less wasteful than ordinary bulbs because they do not get so hot.

Electrical circuits

A **conductor** allows electricity to flow. An **insulator** prevents the flow of electricity.

Danger!
The plastic insulation on wires in the home prevents you from touching the wires inside.

Electrons are part of an atom. They are tiny particles. Trillions of them will flow in a circuit.

A battery is really a group of cells joined together.

Conductors and insulators

All materials can be classified as conductors or insulators of electricity.

Good conductors	Moderate	Poor	Insulators
all the metals e.g.	silicon	water	wood
gold	germanium		plastic
silver	carbon		rubber
copper			glass
iron			dry air
aluminium			pottery

Testing circuit

A simple circuit like this can be used to test whether a material is a conductor or insulator.

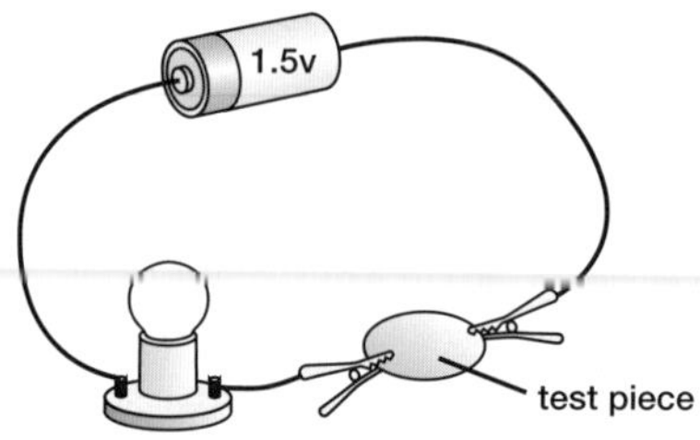

Electrical symbols

In any circuit diagram the following symbols are used:

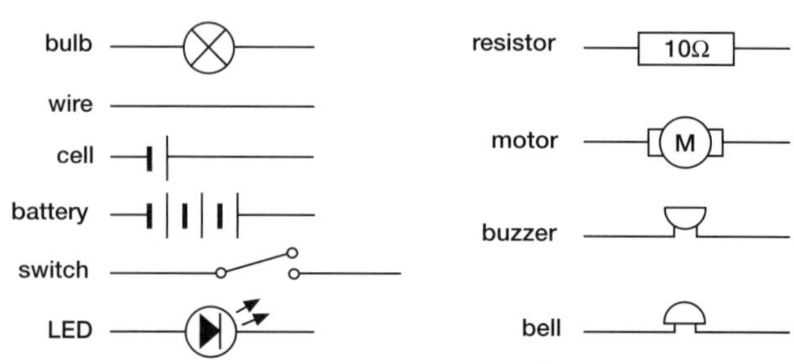

Looking at a bulb in detail

Bulbs are made to resist the flow of electricity. The filament is very thin. This means that the electricity has to struggle to get through the wire. This is called resistance. As it does so, the filament becomes hot as the electrons in the electrical flow bump into the atoms of the wire.

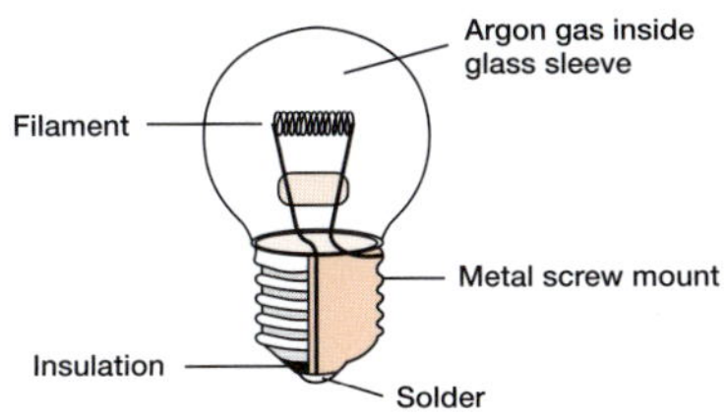

All filament bulbs work in this way, even the ones in your home. Fluorescent tubes and long-life bulbs work in a different way.

Measuring current flow

We use an ammeter to measure the flow of electricity. In most circuits using a battery, the flow of electricity will probably be about 0.5 amps. Ammeters measure the number of electrons passing through them.

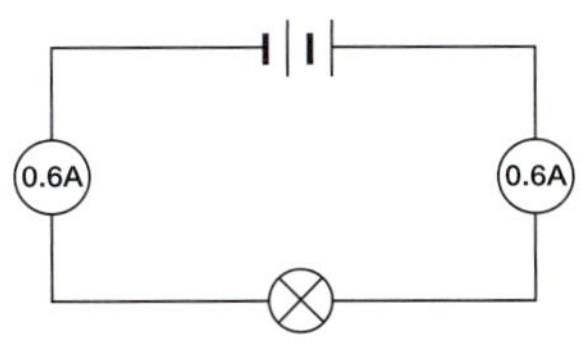

The two ammeters measure the same flow. This means that the same flow comes into the bulb as leaves it.

If the ammeters recorded different current flow, some of the electrons would have gone missing!

Series circuits

This is a circuit where there are three bulbs in series. The resistance of all three bulbs is combined and makes it difficult for the electricity to flow. This means that each bulb glows dimly. If any of the bulbs is unscrewed, the other bulbs will go out as there is no longer a complete circuit.

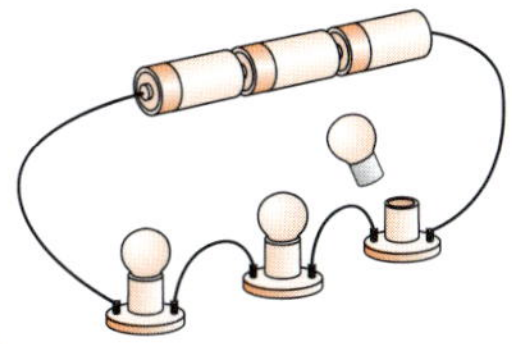

This circuit has two cells in series. This means that there will be twice as much electrical flow as with only one cell. The bulb or bulbs will glow more brightly.

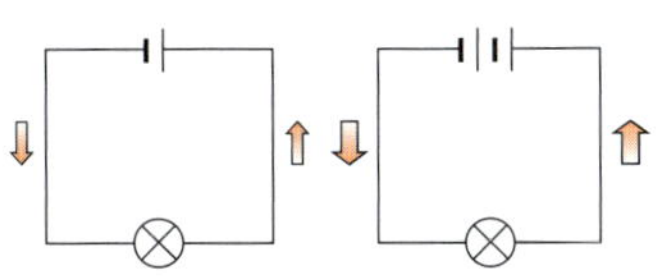

Parallel circuits

All the circuits in your home are **parallel**. This means that turning on a light in one room does not affect the lights in the rest of the house. The same is true of the sockets on the wall.

On the bottom of the opposite page you can see that when the bulbs are different the flow in each part of the circuit might be different.

What is a parallel circuit?

This is a parallel circuit. Notice that the current can flow through either of the two branches. This means that if you disconnect one bulb, the other will carry on glowing. This is unlike the series circuit.

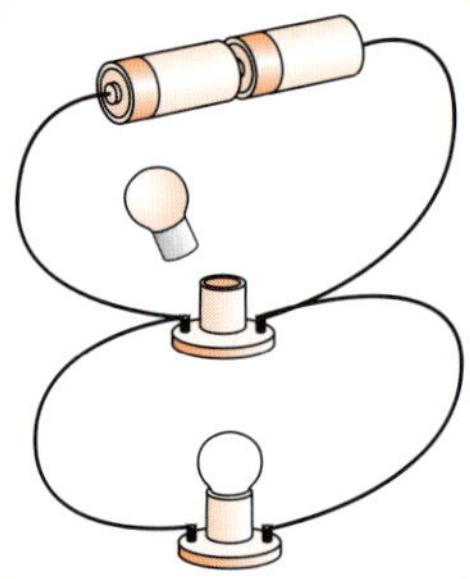

Current flow in parallel circuit

If the flow from the battery is 3 amps it must be the same as it returns to the battery (see page 38).

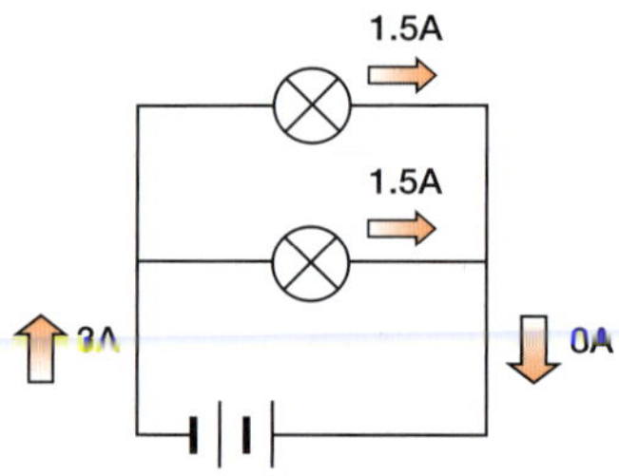

The current splits evenly when it comes to the identical bulbs. This means that there is a flow of 1.5 amps through each bulb. When they rejoin the total flow is 3 amps.

Switches

Switches break the circuit. In the parallel circuits at the top of the next page there are four switches. In which circuit

- ★ is bulb A only lit? ______________________
- ★ is bulb B only lit? ______________________
- ★ is neither bulb lit? ______________________
- ★ are both bulbs lit? ______________________

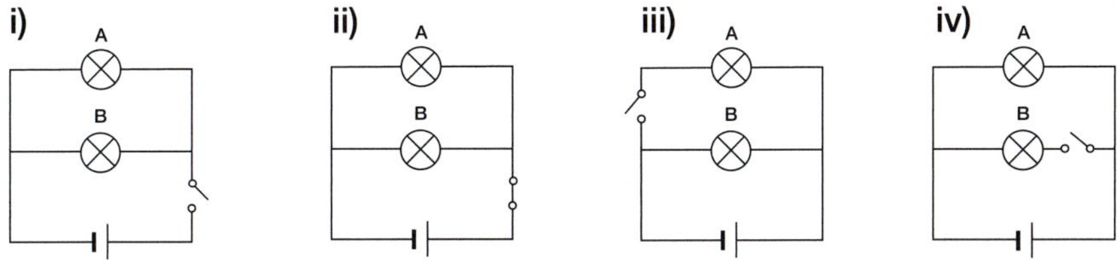

Some puzzles

1. Which bulb will glow most brightly?

2. What will be the current flowing at the places marked with a question mark?

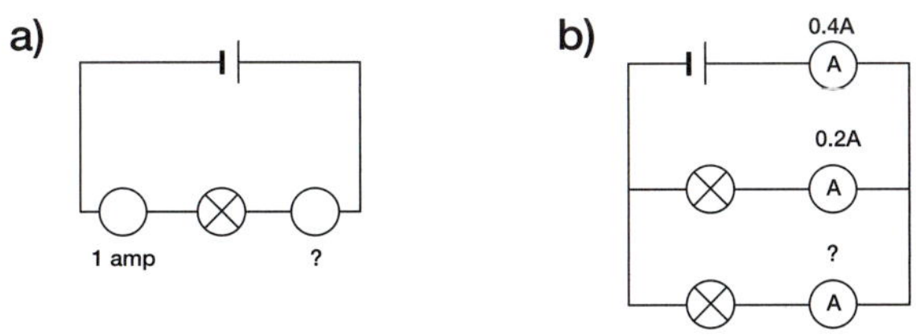

More parallel circuits

Where the bulbs in each part of the parallel circuit are different there will be a different size of flow through them. In the circuit below the current leaving the battery and the current returning are the same. In the two parallel parts of the circuit the flow is different with more going through one bulb than the other.

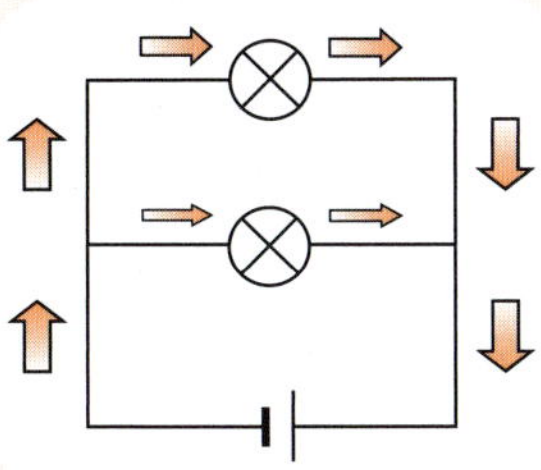

These examples assume that the bulbs in each part of the circuit are equal.

Voltage and components

Potential difference

You might hear the term potential difference (p.d.). This means much the same as **voltage**.

Energy changes

Look at the section on energy changes (page 36). In a battery the chemical energy is converted into electrical energy which is turned into light and heat in a bulb.

Remember!

The **flow** or **current** is the same on both sides. It is only the difference in the **energy** that the voltmeter measures.

Batteries

Batteries provide the energy for the electrical flow. The electrons enter the battery having done work going round the circuit. As they leave the battery the electrons are supplied with electrical energy by the battery.

The chemical reaction in the battery supplies the electrical energy. The energy is converted into work when the flow of electricity has to push through the filament.

There are chemicals inside a battery that react together to produce a flow of current. Once all the chemicals have reacted in this way the battery cannot supply a flow of electricity. Rechargeable batteries use electricity from the mains to reverse this reaction.

Torches

Torches use one, two or three batteries. Those with three batteries are normally brighter than those with one because the voltage of the batteries is added together.

1 battery = 1.5 volts 2 batteries = 3 volts 3 batteries = 4.5 volts

Measuring voltage

Electrical energy is measured using a voltmeter. The voltmeter is connected parallel (page 40) to a component in the circuit. The voltmeter measures the difference in the energy between the electricity going into the component and the energy of the electricity leaving it.

Examples

In the circuit at the top of the next page we know that the battery supplies 9 volts.

In this circuit all the 9 volts are used in the single bulb.

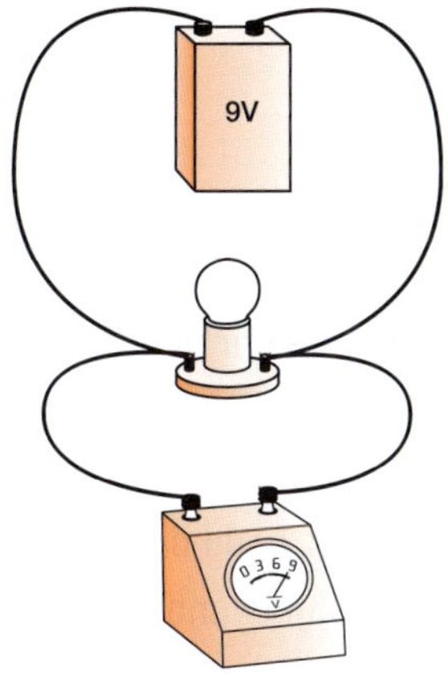

In the circuit below 6 volts are used in the bigger bulb and only 3 volts in the smaller bulb. Notice that the voltage supplied by the battery always equals the voltage used in the circuit.

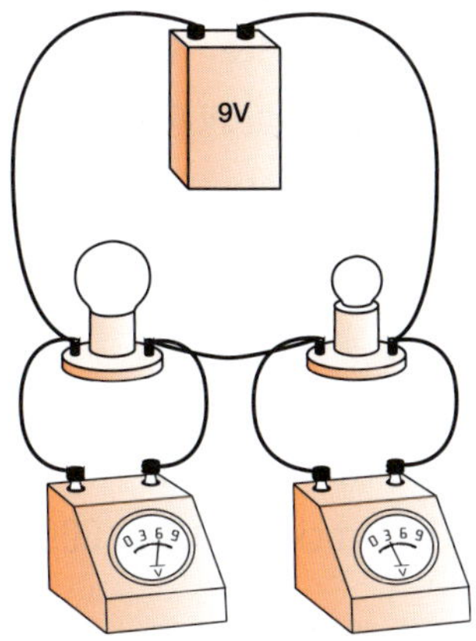

LED

The small red warning lights on electrical items you see all over your house are in fact light emitting diodes (LED). You can also see LEDs light up in the back window of cars as they brake. These devices have a very high resistance. This means that they make it difficult for electricity to flow in a circuit. They use very little electricity and are a very efficient way of producing light.

Light Dependent Resistors (LDR)

These devices do not let electricity flow when it is dark. They do let electricity flow when it is light. They are used to switch on lights at night using an electronic circuit.

LEDs are so efficient that they are now used to produce bright lights on bikes and some traffic lights (normally green arrows).

It seems the wrong way round but the electronic circuits cleverly use the LDR to do this.

Pulls and pushes

Forces make things change shape, speed up or change direction.

Forces

Examples of forces include:

- pushes or pulls made by people or machines
- the pull from a magnet
- the pull of gravity
- the pull of a stretched elastic band or spring
- friction between a moving object and a surface
- air resistance

Measuring forces

The unit used to measure force is the newton (N). The easiest way to measure force is using a spring balance. The amount that the spring is stretched is equal to the force needed to move the object.

The unit of force is named after the great scientist **Sir Isaac Newton**.

- Force needed to push a book across the table = 0.5 N
- Pull of gravity on an apple = 1 N
- Force needed to push open a door = 3 N
- Pull of gravity on you = 60 N
- Push from the wheels of a car = 3000 N
- Push from the engines of a rocket = 1,000,000 N

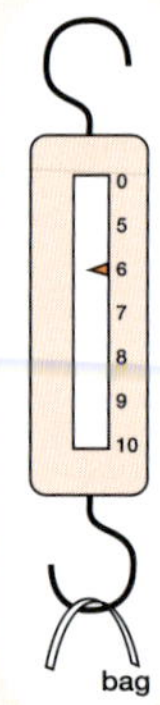

All these figures are approximate. You can measure them if you have a spring balance.

Gravity

The force of gravity pulls all objects to the Earth. Weight is the name given to the pull of gravity on an object. Near the Earth's surface the pull of gravity on 1 kg is 10 N. On the Moon the pull of gravity is less, so you would weigh less.

On the massive planets of the solar system you would weigh even more than you do on Earth.

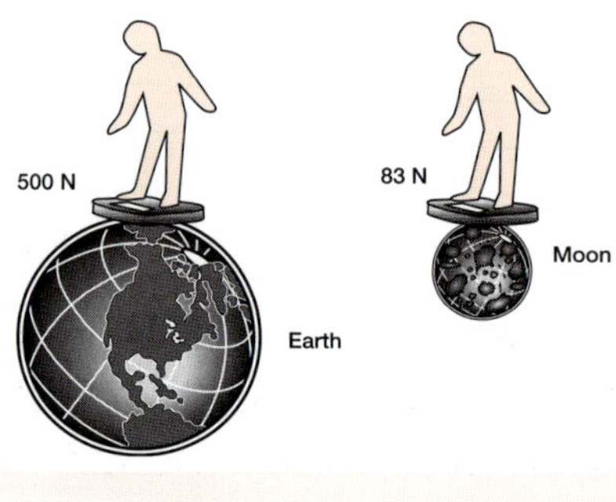

Falling with gravity

Do heavy things fall faster than light ones? Take two different things, such as a cushion and a paperclip, or a small ball and a large ball. Let them go from the same height.
Which hits the ground first or do they land together?

In the 17th Century the Italian scientist **Galileo** was supposed to have tried this experiment from the Leaning Tower of Pisa using a musket ball and a cannonball.

Stretching with gravity

If you put weights on a spring or elastic band it will stretch as gravity pulls it.

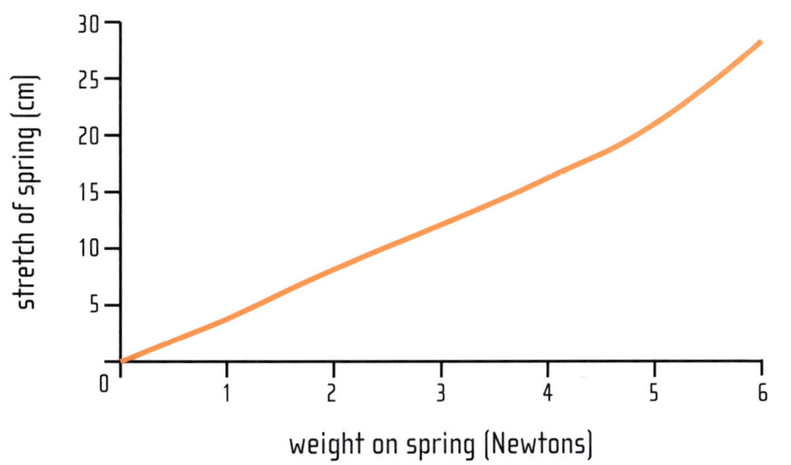

The stretch of the spring increases as weight is added. What happens when 5 N is reached? Does the same pattern continue all the way through?

Friction

The force of friction works against moving objects. If you try to drag a bag across the floor you will notice that it is harder on carpet than on a smooth tiled floor.

Lubrication using oil reduces friction in engines by forming a liquid layer between the rubbing surfaces.

Try this...

Rub your hands together quite quickly. You will notice that they become warm. This is because friction causes them to heat up.

Stability

Get two or three empty plastic drinks bottles. Put a different amount of water in each and put a lid on. Experiment with the stability of the bottles. Which of them topples most easily and which is hardest to push over?

It all depends where the centre of gravity is. If it is very low, it is difficult to make it topple.

Speeding up, slowing down 1

Accelerate means to get faster.

Think about it!

Why do you think athletes wear skin tight clothes when sprinting? If they had flapping clothes what effect would that have?

Did you know...?

Parachutes fall at a constant speed after they have slowed from the freefall part of the drop.

More about forces

When a ball is sitting still on the ground all the forces acting on it are balanced.

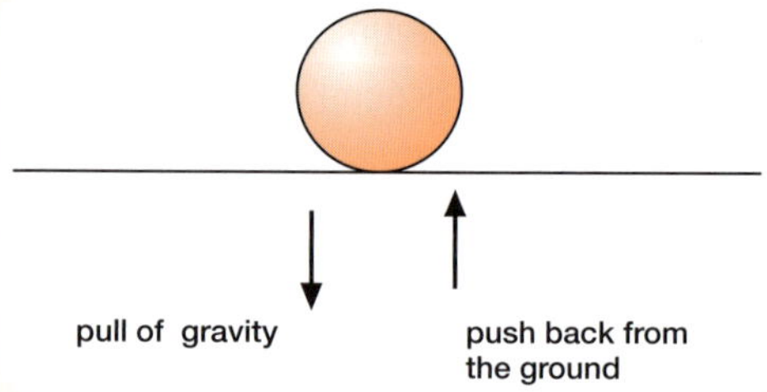

When it gets kicked the forces are unbalanced and the ball accelerates.

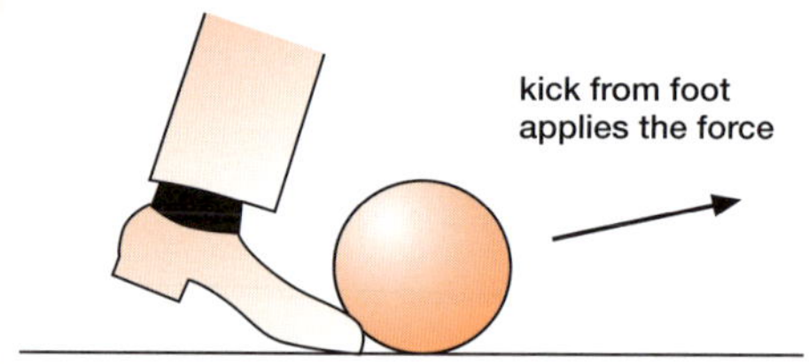

Once it leaves the foot it is slowing down all the time. The forces of friction and air resistance slow it down.

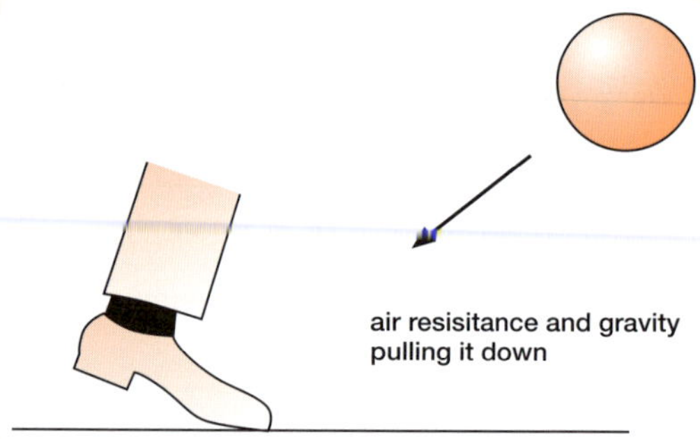

Air resistance

Air resistance is the force that slows moving objects as they travel through the air. Air builds up in front of the moving object. This air has to be pushed out of the way as the object moves.

This is a quick experiment to give you the feel of air resistance. Screw up a ball of scrap paper really tight and kick it across the room. Now get another piece and screw it up less tightly. Kick this one. It won't go so far because there is more air resistance working against the larger ball.

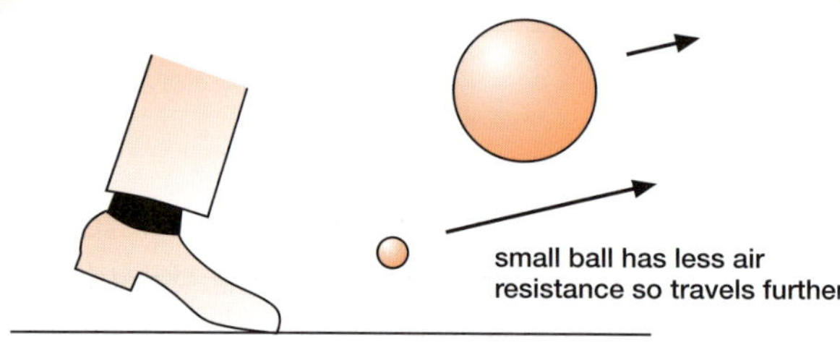

Falling really slowly

Get a small piece of cottonwool or some kind of fluff. Drop it. How quickly does it fall? Now tease it out so that it has an even bigger surface area. Drop it again. Do you notice that it now drops really slowly? Notice that it falls at a constant speed.

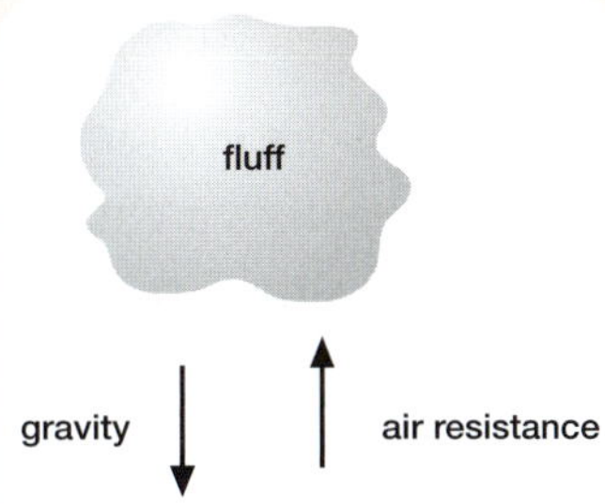

The forces are equal because the cottonwool was already falling when the two forces became equal.

Air brakes

Large lorries have much more air resistance than cars. They try to reduce this by using a special shape above the cab to help them cut through the air more easily. Experiment with changing air resistance on some toy cars.

Try this

Make a ramp for them to run down. Cut some card to make air brakes of different sizes. Use sticky tape to fix them on the cars. What effect does changing the size of the card air brake have on the distance the car travels off the ramp?

Work out the area (length x width) of the card and write it in a table.

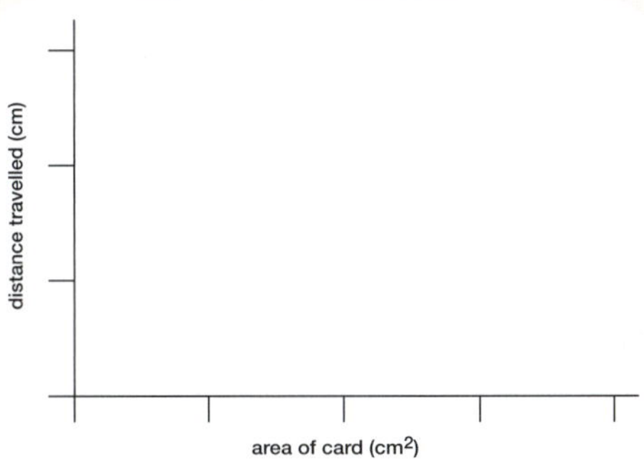

Designed for speed!

Racing cars and sports cars are really streamlined so they can cut through the air easily.

Record your data on a table and complete this graph.

Speeding up, slowing down 2

There are 60 seconds in one minute and 300 seconds in five minutes.

Speed

When you are in a car you will notice that speed is measured in miles per hour. Scientists prefer to measure speed in metres per second (m/s). Here are some speeds of moving things.

Object	Speed
Snail	0.0005 m/s
Person walking	2 m/s
Person sprinting	10 m/s
Train	60 m/s
Jet airliner	400 m/s

The formula for working out average speed is to divide the distance travelled (d) by the time taken (t).

$$\text{average speed} = \frac{\text{distance travelled}}{\text{time taken}} = \frac{d}{t}$$

For example a person jogging might cover 900 m in five minutes.

$$\text{average speed} = \frac{900}{300} = 3 \text{ m/s}$$

Work out how fast a person is running if they cover 1200 metres in 5 minutes.

Try to find the length that the pendulum needs to be to swing once per second.

Pendulums

Make a pendulum from a length of cotton and a small weight. Hang it from a stick weighted down with heavy books.

How many swings does your pendulum do in 15 seconds?

Make the pendulum longer and see how many swings it does in 15 seconds now.

Shorten the pendulum and see what effect that has.

Complete a table like this:

Length of pendulum	Number of swings in 15 seconds
5 cm	
10 cm	
20 cm	
40 cm	
60 cm	

Show axes of line graph
horiz = length
vertical axis = number of swings

Draw a line graph using the data you have collected.

Rope slides

Holding on to a handle and whizzing down a rope is great fun. The force of gravity pulls you down the slide. The forces of air resistance and friction are working against your movement.

To go faster, make sure you do not have any flapping clothes and use a slippery rope tied at a steep angle.

To go slower, have a coat that catches the air and use a rope that is rough and tied at a shallow slope.

Remember, rope slides can be dangerous! Never try this without expert supervision.

Try it yourself

- Tie a length of cotton in a safe place.
- Bend a paperclip to act as a hook.
- Tape a small toy to the hook.
- Slide it down the cotton.
- Change the speed it moves at by altering the air resistance and the friction on the toy. You can alter the effect of gravity by changing the angle.

Make sure that people can't walk into the cotton and hurt themselves.

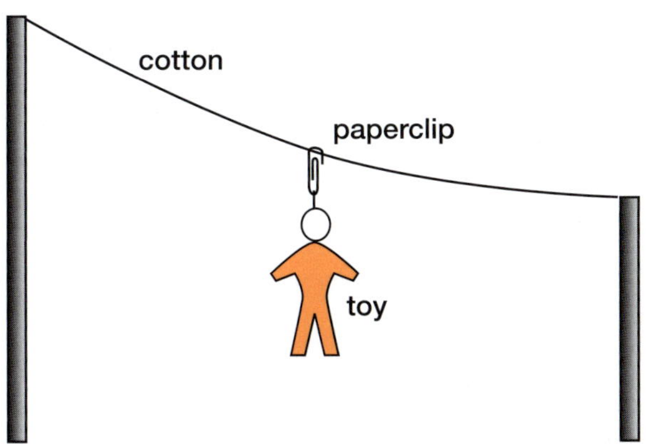

Floating forces

Floating party balloons are filled with **helium**, which is a gas less dense than air.

Plimsoll line

The plimsoll line is painted on surface ships to show the level to which they can be safely loaded.

Even a 100,000 tonne ship has to **displace** its own weight of water. It is the volume below the water that is responsible for displacing such huge weights of water.

Floating

When you float in water the force of gravity is balanced by the upthrust from the water.

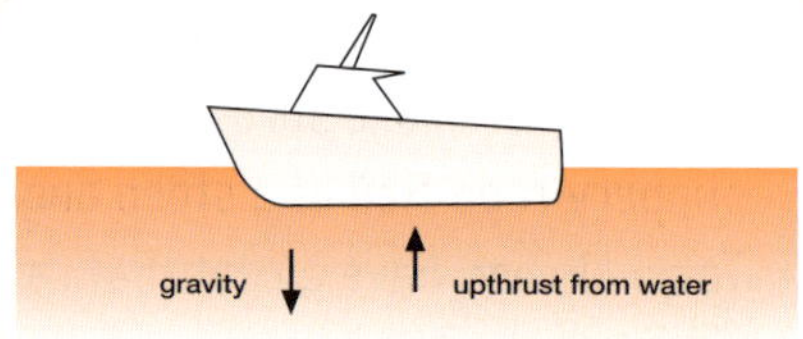

When a hot air balloon or a party balloon floats in the air the forces of upthrust from the air and gravity are equal. If you have a helium-filled party balloon, add or take away paperclips so that it just hovers in the air.

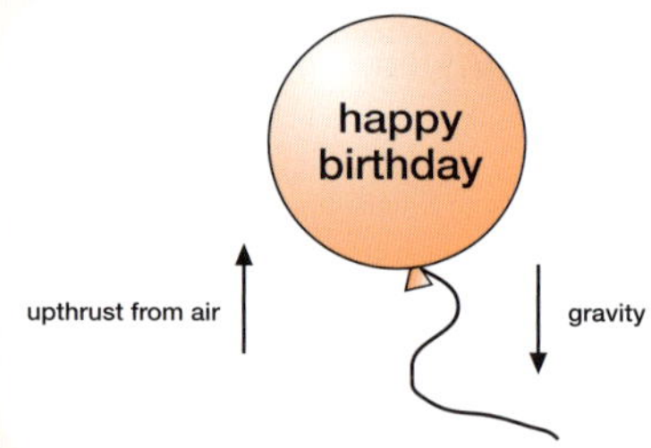

The forces on a submarine

A submarine floats on the surface of the water.
When it dives it floods its tanks so that it becomes heavier. If it is on the bottom and it wants to float to the surface, it pushes water out of its tanks and so becomes lighter.
These diagrams show the forces on the submarine.

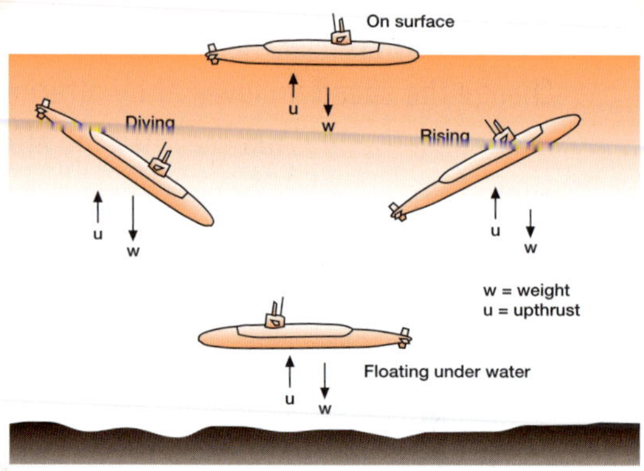

Why do objects float?

Look at the diagram at the top of the next page.
Take a beaker with some water in it and mark the level of the water.
Put a ball or other object that will float into the beaker.
Notice what happens to the level of the water.
Floating objects displace water. The weight of water the object displaces is the same as its own weight.

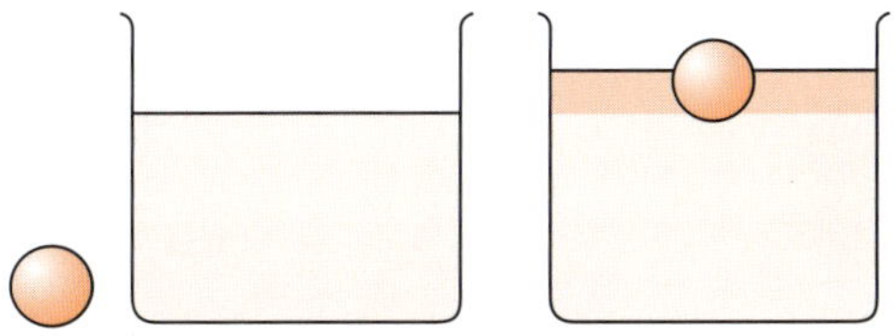

This amount of water weighs the same as the floating ball.

Make an egg float

Take two identical clear glasses big enough to hold an egg. Put water in both of them. Add four dessertspoons of salt to the water in one of the containers and dissolve it all. The egg will probably sink in the fresh water but float in the salty water. The same will probably be true of a piece of soap.

This happens because salt water is denser (see page 25) than fresh water. The upthrust the egg gets from the fresh water is not enough to make it float. Salt water is denser than fresh water so it gives more upthrust to the egg.

Bobbing sultanas

Pour a glass of fizzy drink. Before drinking it, put a couple of sultanas or raisins in the drink. Watch them rise up as they get bubbles on them. The sultanas will sink again once all their bubbles burst.

Remember!

The weight of one cubic centimetre of water is exactly 1 gram.

Your egg may or may not float – it all depends how much salt you add.

The Earth in space

Sundials are normally outside but this indoor one works just as well.

Look in the papers or on TV weather forecasts for the actual time of sunrise or sunset each day. All these times are **GMT** and have not been changed for summertime when clocks go forward by one hour.

Did you know...?

Some people think that summer happens because we get closer to the Sun. That cannot be correct because how could the Australians have summer if that was how it worked?

Day and night

The Earth turns on its axis once each day. This is why the Sun appears to move across the sky. Track the movement of the Earth using a shadow stick. Do this by standing a pencil in some blu-tack on a piece of paper. Draw the shadow of the stick at different times during the day.

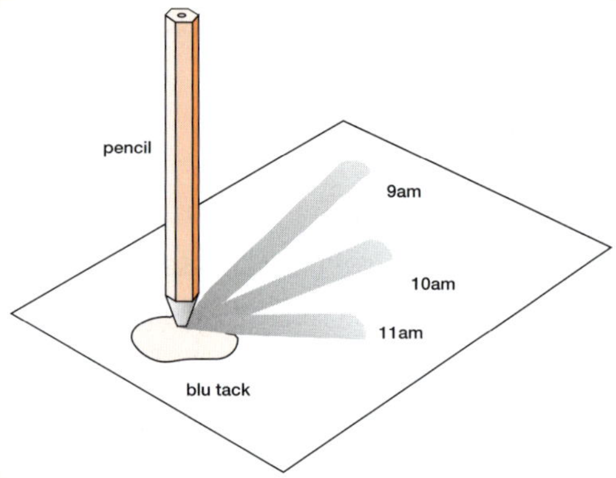

This table shows the approximate times of sunrise and sunset. It is for Britain for the middle of each month. Calculate the length of the average day for each month. Draw a line graph using your information.

	sunrise (am)	sunset (pm)	length of day
January	8.00	4.20	
February	7.15	5.05	
March	6.15	6.05	
April	5.00	7.00	
May	4.10	8.45	
June	3.45	8.20	
July	4.00	8.10	
August	4.45	7.20	
September	5.35	6.15	
October	6.25	5.10	
November	7.20	4.10	
December	8.00	3.50	

Orbit of the Earth

The Earth's orbit around the Sun is roughly circular. It takes approximately 365 days to orbit the Sun. The seasons occur because the Earth is tilted at 23.5°. The diagram at the top of the next page shows that the northern hemisphere is tilted towards the Sun in June and tilted away from the Sun in December.

In summer the Sun's warmth is concentrated in a smaller area than in winter when the same amount of heat is spread over a larger area.

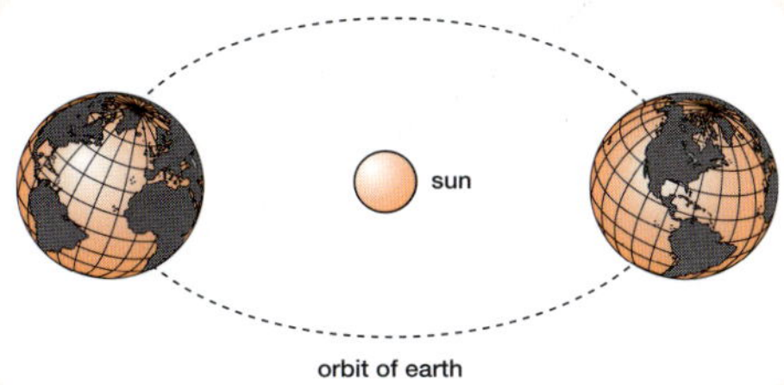

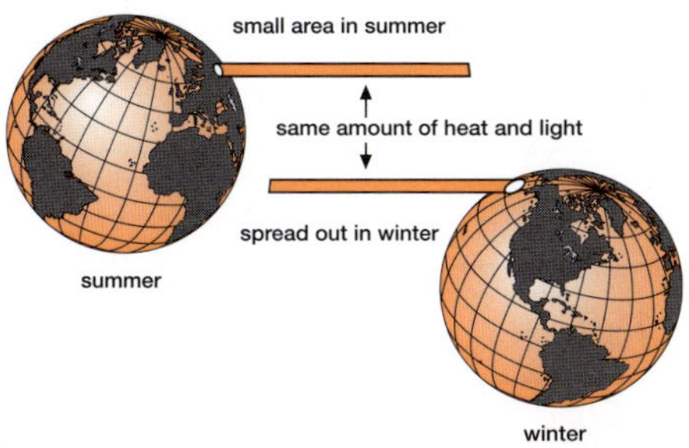

You can see this for yourself if you shine a torch at a globe.

Phases of the Moon

The Moon orbits the Earth approximately once every 28 days. It goes from new moon to new moon in that time. (Confusingly, a new moon is when you cannot see the moon at all.) Make a moon diary of your own by drawing the shape of the Moon each night you see it. Note also the time that the Moon rises and sets. You will see that the Moon rises in the east and sets in the west. This is just like the Sun, since the movement across the sky of the Sun and Moon are both caused by the way the Earth turns.

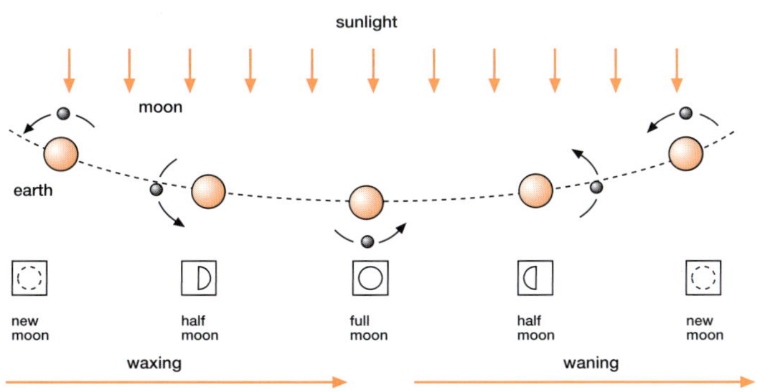

The Moon's surface

The Moon has many craters covering its surface. These were formed by meteorites hitting the surface. You can also see large smooth areas on the Moon's surface. These are called seas. They have no water in them but were formed by enormous lava flows millions of years ago.

Moon data

The Moon is small compared with the Earth. It would take 89 moons to weigh the same as one Earth.

Tides are controlled by the gravitational pull of the Moon (page 44).

The Moon is 384,000 km away from the Earth and orbits at 1 km per second (that's 1000 m/second – see page 48).

The planets

To find the **diameter** of the planets, double the **radius**.

What are the planets made of?

The inner four planets are all rocky. The next four are mainly made from gas. Pluto is a tiny object that many scientists do not think of as a true planet. They think it is an **asteroid**, which was captured by the Sun's gravity long after the **Solar System** was created.

Planets

There are nine planets in the solar system.

	radius of planet (km)	distance from Sun (million km)
Mercury	2000	58
Venus	6000	108
Earth	6000	150
Mars	3000	228
Jupiter	70000	778
Saturn	60000	1427
Uranus	26000	2870
Neptune	24000	4497
Pluto	1500	5900

Planet models

Use these pictures of planets to help you design scale models of the planets to hang from your bedroom ceiling. Use the radius of the planets to help you get the relative sizes right.

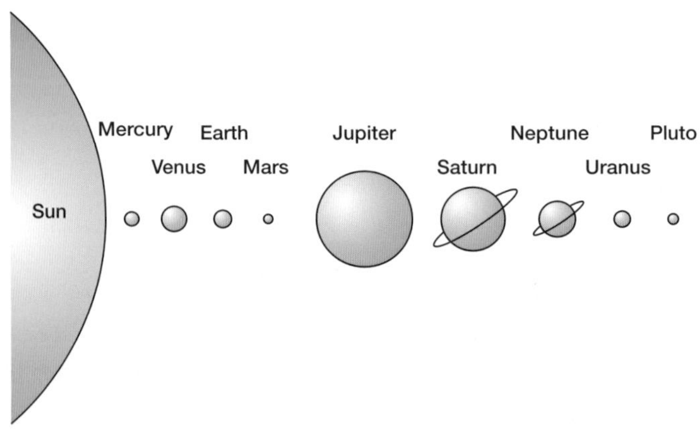

Distance from the Sun

To make a scale model of the planets using discs 4 cm in radius you would need to place the discs many kilometres apart. Instead, use a length of wallpaper and mark the places where the planets are. You will need a 6 m length of wallpaper. Mark Pluto at 590 cm from the Sun.

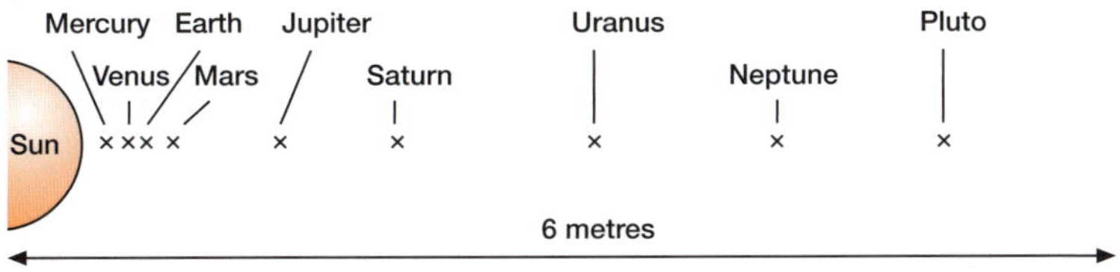

The monster planet

Jupiter is a huge planet. It is over 11 times the size of the Earth. It takes 12 years to orbit the Sun. (It has to travel much further than the Earth as its orbit is so wide.) The temperature on the clouds of Jupiter is about −110 °C. Jupiter's biggest feature is the Great Red Spot, which is a storm 40,000 km across. The Earth would fit into it many times over. Jupiter has at least 16 moons, the largest of which are Io, Europa, Ganymede and Callisto. These four can easily be seen from the Earth using a standard telescope.

The Sun is a light source

The Sun is the centre of the solar system. It is the only light source and the planets only reflect its light. No planets have light of their own. The easiest planet to spot is Venus. You can see it in the west immediately after sunset and in the east at sunrise. The reason why you see Venus in those positions is because it is closer to the Sun than the Earth.

Pole Star

Look in the sky on a dark night. Find the Plough. This is a constellation of seven stars. If you follow the two stars on the right hand side of the Plough you will see a dimmer star called the Pole Star.

Our galaxy

The Sun is just one of billions of stars in our galaxy. You can see the stars of our home galaxy as the Milky Way, which is visible as a stripe of dim stars across the night sky.

Science on the net

Visits to museums

There are many museums you can visit without leaving home. Here are some of them:

www.exploratorium.com
This interactive museum from San Francisco has many involving features.

www.fmnh.org
The Field Museum of Natural History in Chicago has got a great dinosaur exhibit.

www.loc.gov
This is a big one. It is the Library of Congress in Washington DC. This site is full of features to help you do research.

www.nhm.ac.uk
The site of the Natural History Museum in London.

www.ucmp.berkeley.edu/help/timeform.html
The University of California's ride through geological time.

www.seaworld.org
This site has webcams that let you watch feeding time. There are games and quizzes too.

www.ex.ac.uk/bugclub/
How to look after any bugs and crawlies you find.

www.yucky.com
Horrid science for the strong of stomach!

Use search engines

www.fourmmilab.ch/earthview/vplanet.html
See the Earth in real time as it rotates. Look at the way that shadows change as the Earth rotates.

www.nasa.gov
A huge site with all you could possibly want to know about NASA and its work.

http://deepspace.physics.ucsb.edu
Look through a telescope at the universe.

http://space.jpl.nasa.gov
This is a solar system simulator – you can view the solar system from anywhere you like.

Use search engines

If you want to know about a science topic try
www.google.com
In the search box type in the key words for your search. If you want to know about the tides in the seas around Britain type in
tides Britain time
If you want to find out more about Jupiter try typing
Jupiter planet

Glossary

Acid A chemical that forms charged particles of hydrogen in solution.

Acid rain Rain which dissolves gases from the air to form an acid.

Air resistance The force which slows objects moving through the air.

Algae Simple plants which live in very damp places.

Alkali A chemical which forms charged particles of oxygen and hydrogen in solution.

Ammeter A device for measuring electrical flow around a circuit.

Amoeba A single celled animal which moves by pushing out its body.

Amphibian A type of vertebrate which lays its eggs in water.

Antacid A chemical which neutralises acids.

Anther The organ in a flower which produces pollen.

Arachnid The type of arthropod which has eight legs.

Arthropods Invertebrates with jointed limbs.

Asteroids Rocks which move through space.

Atom The smallest particle of an element.

Axis The line around which a sphere rotates. The earth's axis is inclined at 23.5°.

Base Another word for an alkali.

Battery A device which produces a flow of electricity when a chemical reaction takes place.

Cartilage Tissue which stops bones from rubbing together at joints.

Cells The building blocks of living things.

Cell membrane The covering of a cell – the material which keeps the cell's shape.

Cellulose The material from which the cell walls of plants are made.

Chemical energy The form of energy which is stored in the bonds of chemicals. Food is a form of chemical energy.

Chloroplasts The parts of a plant cell which take part in photosynthesis.

Colloid A mixture of a liquid and a solid which does not dissolve in the liquid. The particles in colloids are smaller than those in suspensions. The solid in a colloid cannot be filtered out.

Condensing When a gas turns to a liquid it condenses.

Conduction The process by which heat or electricity passes through a substance.

Conductor This can apply to heat or electricity. Conductors are those substances which let heat or electricity pass easily.

Connective tissue Tissue which supports and connects such as bone, cartilage and fatty tissue.

Consumer An organism which does not produce food itself. All animals are consumers. Green plants are producers.

Crustacean A type of arthropod which has a hard shell and more than eight legs.

Current The flow of electricity is referred to as the current. It is measured in amps.

Cytoplasm The jelly-like liquid inside a cell.

Density Density is the mass per unit volume. Materials with a high density are heavy for their size.

Displacement Displacement is the volume of a liquid which is pushed out of the way by a solid.

Dissolving Solids are dissolved in a liquid when they break down into particles the size of molecules or atoms. The solid and liquid form a solution when the solid dissolves.

Egg The cell produced by the female which grows into a new individual if fertilised by a sperm.

Electrical energy The form of energy which is a flow of electricity.

Electrons Electrons are charged particles which circle the nucleus of an atom.

Emulsion A colloidal mixture of two liquids.

Energy Energy is the ability to do work.

Epithelial cells These form the sheets of cells such as those in skin.

Evaporation Evaporation is the change from a liquid to a gas.

Faeces The solid waste material which is excreted by animals.

Fertilisation The process which takes place when a sperm or pollen meets an ovum or an ovule.

Filament a) Part of a bulb which is made of tungsten.
b) The part of a flower which holds up the anther.

Food chain A way of showing **part** of the feeding relationships in an environment.

Food web A way of showing **all** the feeding relationships in an environment.

Fossil fuels Fuels such as coal, oil and gas which were formed many years ago.

Friction The force which acts against the movement of objects.

Fungus An organism which gets its food from breaking down dead material.

Galaxy A group of billions of stars.

Glycogen A store of sugar.

Gravity The force which pulls two massive objects together.

Greenhouse effect The effect caused by the atmosphere trapping heat.

Gut Another name for the intestines which digest food.

Heat energy The form of energy which hot objects possess.

Hemisphere Half a sphere.

Indicator A chemical which turns colour in the presence of another chemical. Litmus turns red in the presence of an acid.

Insulator a) a material which prevents the flow of electricity.
b) a material which slows the movement of heat.

Kinetic Kinetic refers to movement. Kinetic energy is the energy possessed by moving objects.

LDR A resistor which increases its resistance when it is dark. It decreases resistance when it is light.

LED A device which glows when a small electrical current flows through it.

Lichen An organism which is composed of an alga and a fungus.

Ligament The connective tissue which holds joints together.

Light energy The energy possessed by light. Lasers are a concentrated form of light energy.

Mammals Vertebrates which have hairy skin and feed their young on milk.

Mass Mass is a measurement of the amount of material.

Menstruation The monthly flow of a small amount of blood and an unfertilised egg from the womb.

Microbes Another name for bacteria and viruses.

Mitochondria The energy packs of a cell.

Molecules Groups of atoms.

Molluscs A group of invertebrates which have a hard shell and no jointed limbs.

Moss A type of green plant which reproduces by means of spores.

Muscle The type of tissue which can lengthen and shorten to pull on bones.

Newton The unit which measures force.

Non-renewable energy sources This is another term for fossil fuels.

Nucleus The centre of an atom or cell.

Orbit The motion of one object circling round another object. The earth orbits the Sun.

Organ Part of the body which does a particular job. The heart is the organ which pumps blood.

Organism A living thing. Plants, animals, fungi and bacteria are all organisms.

Ovary The organ which produces eggs.

Ovum An egg cell.

Oxidisation The process which happens when oxygen is combined with another chemical.

Parallel circuit An electrical circuit where there are two pathways.

Pendulum A string with a weight on the end which swings at a regular rate is a form of pendulum.

pH A measure of the acidity of a solution. High pH is alkali and low pH is acid.

Photosynthesis The process by which a plant makes food from carbon dioxide, water and sunlight energy.

Placenta The organ that provides blood to the developing foetus.

Pollination The process of taking pollen to the egg cell in a flower.

Potential energy The energy possessed by objects which are high above the ground.

Producer Plants are producers of food. Animals are consumers of food.

Puberty The time when children turn into adults.

Renewable energy resources These include sunlight, wave power, and wind power.

Reptiles The group of vertebrates with scaly skin which lay eggs on land.

Saturation Solutions are saturated when the liquid cannot dissolve any more solid.

Self-fertilisation Flowers which transfer pollen from their own anthers to their own stigma and then fertilise their own ovules are fertilising themselves.

Series circuit An electrical circuit where the electricity must flow down a single pathway.

Solar system The Solar System consists of the Sun and all nine planets and asteroids.

Solute This is the name for the solid which is dissolved to form a solution.

Solvent This is the name for the liquid which dissolves the solid to form a solution.

Sperm The male sex cell which fertilises the female's egg cell.

Spinal cord The long cord of nerve cells which runs from the brain down through the backbone to the bottom of the back.

Spore The reproductive cell produced by mosses and ferns. It is similar in some ways to a seed in flowering plants.

Stamen The male part of the flower which includes the anther and filament.

Stigma The sticky part of the top of the female organs in a flower. It traps pollen before fertilisation takes place.

Strain energy The form of energy possessed by stretched objects. A stretched elastic band has strain energy.

Style The style is the part of the flower which connects the stigma and the ovary.

Suspension A suspension is similar to a colloid but in a suspension the solid particles are much larger and can be filtered out.

Switch A device which makes and breaks an electrical circuit to allow electricity to flow or to stop it flowing.

Tendon The connective tissue which attached muscles to bone.

Tissue Body tissue is made from groups of similar cells. Muscle tissue is made from muscle cells.

Vacuole The space in a cell – in plants this is much larger than in animals.

Vertebrates The group of animals such as mammals, birds and fish which have a backbone and a bony skeleton.

Voltage The measure of electrical energy.

Answers

Reproduction and growing up *(p 11)*

In spring there is plenty of food and longer days to look for food to feed young. Summer follows spring so it is easier for young to find food to build themselves up for the winter.

Growth of a baby *(p 13)*

Humans spend a long time learning skills and knowledge from their parents and teachers.

Plant reproduction *(p 14)*

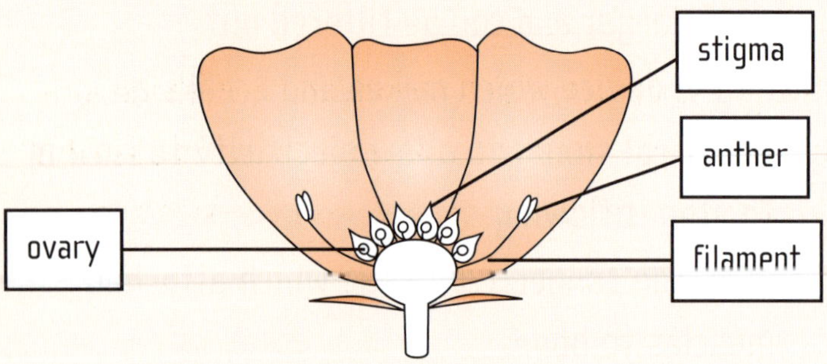

buttercup

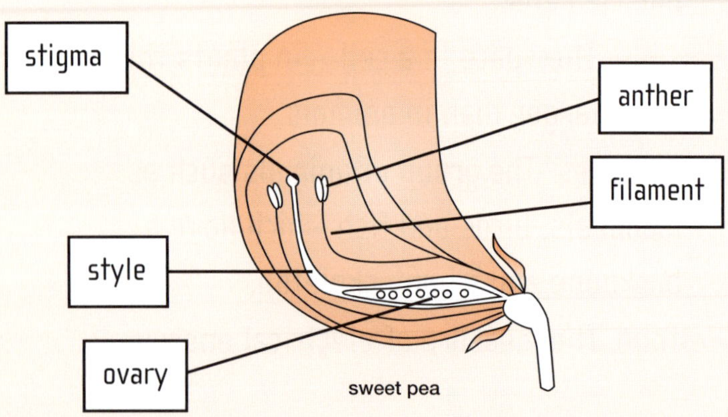

sweet pea

The style on the buttercup is very short.

Animals with backbones *(p 19)*

Odd ones out:

★ shark (it is a fish the others are mammals)

★ bat (it is a mammal the others are birds)

★ frog (it is an amphibian the others are reptiles)

★ eel (it is a fish the others are reptiles)

Animals without backbones *(p 21)*

All insects have three sections: head, thorax and abdomen. The legs are joined to the thorax.

Fungi and green plants *(p 22)*

Moulds grow more rapidly in fairly warm conditions than they do in cold conditions. Most living processes have an optimum temperature at which they work best. In freezing conditions growth is very slow, and very few living things can grow at all when the temperatures are above boiling point.

Classifying materials *(p 25)*

Try to collect aluminium (very light and quite soft e.g. can), steel (more dense and stronger e.g. spoon), gold (very dense and soft e.g. ring), silver (not as dense as gold), lead (not as dense as gold but denser than steel e.g. old pipes or old fishing weights – not used in modern weights as it is poisonous).

Metals *(p 29)*

Pennies and two penny pieces made before 1990 are non magnetic. Those made later in the 90s are magnetic as the mint changed the formula. This was because the scrap value of the older coins was getting close to their face value.

Chemical changes *(p 32)*

You will have to decide which methods slows down the reactions best. It will depend on many factors in the particular experiment you try.

Parallel circuits *(p 40)*

★ Bulb A lit: iv

★ Only bulb B lit: iii

★ Neither lit: i

★ Both lit: ii

★ 1 b will glow most brightly as there is only one bulb resisting the flow of electricity so more current will flow.

★ 2a The current will be 1 amp as the flow of current is the same at all places in the circuit.

★ 2b 0.2amps as the current splits with half going down one pathway and half going down the other pathway.

Pulls and pushes *(p 45)*

Light and heavy objects fall at the same rate. This is so long as the light object is not very light and does not have a large surface area. Objects like feathers and sheets of paper are so light and have such a large surface area that air resistance masks the effects of gravity.

The graph will show a sudden increase in the length of the spring with only small additions of mass. This happens when the spring becomes over-stretched.

Timetable

Time	Monday	Tuesday	Wednesday	Thursday	Friday
BREAK TIME					
LUNCH TIME					
BREAK TIME					

Notes